G000082455

Evaluating the Primary School

Resources in Education

Other titles in this Series:

Beyond the Core Curriculum, Mike Harrison (editor)

The Language of Discipline, William Rogers

Local Management of Schools, Brent Davies & Chris Braund

Managing the Primary School Budget, Brent Davies & Linda Ellison

Managing Stress in Schools, Sue Ralph & Marie Brown

Marketing the Primary School, Brian Hardie

The School Library: Responding to Change, Elizabeth King

The School Meals Service, Nan Berger

Resources in Education

Evaluating the Primary School

A practical guide to the evaluation process

Brian Hardie MA DLC

Northcote House

This book is dedicated to Chris Braund who died on 5th November 1991 after a fight against cancer.

Chris Braund will be missed, not only as a colleague, an author and a fund of knowledge, but also as a friend who will be in my thoughts constantly.

ISBN 0 7463 0647 4

British Library Cataloguing-in-Publication Data
A catalogue record for this book is available
from the British Library

First published in 1995 by Northcote House Publishers Ltd,
Plymbridge House, Estover Road, Plymouth PL6 7PZ, United Kingdom.
Tel: Plymouth (0752) 735251. Fax: (0752) 695699. Telex: 45635.

Typeset by Kestrel Data, Exeter
Printed and bound in Great Britain by BPC Wheatons, Exeter

Contents

Preface

Evaluation is an activity in which all those in education take part at some time or other whether it is a major evaluation of the whole school or whether it is looking at how successful, or otherwise, was today's teaching.

THE NEED FOR THIS BOOK

There is a need for this particular book on managing evaluation for the following reasons:

- Since the 1988 Education Act and the introduction of OFSTED there has been an even greater emphasis on evaluation in general in schools. This has resulted from School Development Plans which may have included 'Where are we now?' and 'Where do we want to be?' sections. Consequently there is a need to evaluate the school to find out the answers to these questions by **Heads, teachers and governors**.
- The introduction of the National Curriculum has meant **teachers** are evaluating their performance in the classroom in a more precise way.
- Increased accountability, especially for **governors**, has meant that they are having to evaluate the school. They often have little experience in doing this and would benefit from a handbook giving ideas on how this might be done.
- **Parents** have greater choice about the school to which they send their children. They too may have little experience to enable them to do this and would benefit from this handbook.

This is not an 'academic' work. Consequently, it does not follow the 'academic' convention of giving all the sources within each paragraph. These have been left out in order to make the text more readable.

As a further simplification the works and ideas of a variety of authors have been pulled together to make lists which may involve many sources.

The language used has been kept as simple as possible and an attempt has been made at avoiding jargon wherever possible.

The book includes a large number of activities and checklists and is therefore essentially a practical book aimed at teachers, Headteachers, parents and governors.

Three assumptions have been made about those conducting an evaluation in school:

- they are unlikely to have any funding
- they are unlikely to be 'trained' evaluators
- they do want to find out what is *really* happening in the school.

THE CONTENT OF THE BOOK

The first chapter is concerned with the 'theory' and the basic principles of evaluation: this includes definitions. This section of the book, which may be more difficult to read, should help the reader to put evaluation into context. The chapter is succeeded by activities which may help the reader to apply these principles in a more practical manner.

The second chapter begins by considering accountability and development followed by constraints. In the main this chapter is devoted to a synopsis and comment on twelve different methods of whole school evaluation. The chapter concludes with some of the issues which have not been previously considered.

For most teachers the chapter on classroom based evaluation is the most practical of all. As many different techniques as possible have been offered in order to assist classroom teachers to evaluate their own practice where it matters—in the classroom. The information will be of use to others such as Headteachers, governors and parents as it also applies to their *management* of the evaluation of this area of the school.

Evaluation is not a worthwhile activity unless it includes **action**. Chapter four is concerned with the *management* of this most important aspect of evaluation and helps to provide the management techniques to achieve the evaluation cycle of the school. Items which have been included elsewhere in the book are re-examined within this context in this chapter. An example is given of a National Curriculum Plan and the chapter finishes with activities.

The concluding chapter aims to bring things together and this leads to the glossary of terms used, further reading, and an index.

Acknowledgements

I should like to thank many of the staff and students at the Centre for Education Management at Crewe+Alsager Faculty of Manchester Metropolitan University for their help in refining the ideas and format of this book, in particular Tony Devlin.

In addition I should like to thank Roland Seymour for his editorial work on the various drafts of this book and also Derek Swetnam and Glynn Kirkham who did such an excellent job of proof reading.

1
The Context for Evaluation

This chapter is about understanding the basic principles of evaluation and begins with definitions. This is followed by a consideration of the basic elements of evaluation. These elements are all concerned with the questions which need to be asked and the decisions made prior to, during, and subsequent to an evaluation in an educational institution. The sections on criteria for judgement, voluntary or imposed and internal or external are brought together in the section with three approaches to evaluation which is longer than the other sections and may be rather more 'academic' with some 'heavy' words and concepts. This may also be said of the methods element which has included within it a section on styles of evaluation. The final part of this chapter concerns the human factors of evaluation.

The areas which will be considered are:

- Definitions
- Purpose
- Focus and emphasis
- Criteria for judgement
- Voluntary or imposed
- Internal or external
- Three approaches to evaluation
- Methods
- Styles of evaluation
- Organisation and planning
- Resources
- Time
- Reporting
- Control and availability of the information
- Effectiveness of the exercise (evaluation of the evaluation)

- Application and use of the evaluation
- Human factors of evaluation.

DEFINITIONS

The definitions used throughout this book are based on those used by HMI in their book *Quality in Schools: Evaluation and Appraisal.*

EVALUATION

Evaluation is seen as a **general term** to describe **any activity** within the school where the **quality** of what is happening is the subject. This may or may not be systematic. It may involve quantitative descriptions, that is measurement in one form or another. On the other hand, it may involve qualitative descriptions, which concentrate on the qualities and do not include measurement. It is also likely to include value judgements which we ourselves, or others, place on these descriptions.

REVIEW

Review indicates a **retrospective activity** and implies the collection and examination of evidence and information. When this has been completed, however, it is hoped and expected that there will be some action and change as a result of the review. This is particularly the case in chapter three when whole school review is considered in some detail.

APPRAISAL

Appraisal emphasises the forming of qualitative judgements about an activity, a person or an organisation. In schools, however, the term is now assumed, in the minds of some teachers, to have negative connotations connected with personal performance. This term will therefore be used as little as possible because of this potential misunderstanding.

ASSESSMENT

Assessment implies the use of measurement and/or grading based on known criteria. It is therefore usually quantitative, precise and acceptable when used in relation to children but once again it may have negative connotations when linked with teachers.

Many of the questions in this section are taken from Harlen and Elliotts' checklist for planning an evaluation in McCormick, R.,

Calling Education to Account. Their list has been re-ordered, re-grouped, and added to, although many of the questions themselves remain in their original form.

PURPOSE

Purpose is an essential element in any evaluation and needs to be considered before any other. There are two sets of questions to be asked which will be taken in turn. The questions are:

- **what** is the purpose of the evaluation?
- **who** are the people who want the evaluation to be carried out?

WHAT is the purpose of the evaluation? Is it to improve the functioning of the school as a whole or a part of it? Is it in response to a specific problem or issue? Is it for development purposes inside the school or for accountability reasons? What events have caused the evaluation to be needed? Why are we carrying out the evaluation? These are the type of questions which need to be asked, not only by those who are managing the evaluation, but also by those carrying it out.

What are the objectives of the evaluation? Objectives should be SMART and MAC FEW OI!

SMART

- **S**pecific
- **M**easurable
- **A**ttainable
- **R**ealistic
- **T**ime constrained.

Specific

Objectives should be as specific as possible. It is very easy to be vague. One objective for the evaluation may not be enough, so it may be that a set of specific objectives are needed.

Measurable

If objectives are not measurable how will we know when the evaluation has been completed? Measurable objectives have not been a part of the culture of many schools in the past although they are fast becoming a part of the schools of the future. It is often difficult to make educational objectives measurable, so it may be that the measures used are sometimes subjective in their nature, although this is to be discouraged.

Attainable
The objectives must be attainable as otherwise everybody concerned will get discouraged and lose heart.

Realistic
The objectives need to be as realistic as possible. This is similar to the previous point, but it is very easy for an evaluation to become an exercise as opposed to something which is worthwhile. The objectives must be realistic within the constraints of the available time, resources and bearing in mind all the other activities which are happening in the school.

Time constrained
If the objectives are not time-constrained the evaluation will either be rushed or drag on for ever. This balance is not easy to achieve, for while there is a need to keep the momentum going, there is also a need for pacing over the whole evaluation. The second approach to objectives has the acronym MAC FEW OI!

MAC FEW OI!
- **M**easurable within **A**ny **C**onstraints
- **A**chievable
- **C**hallenging

FEW IN NUMBER
- **F**lexible
- **E**asily
- **W**ritten

OI! Do it now!
- **O**rganisational
- **I**ndividual

MAC

Measurable

All objectives **must** be measurable. This is what separates an objective from an aim. These measures should be as 'objective' as is possible rather than 'subjective'. This is often easier said than done, particularly in education, as it can be difficult to give all objectives a numerical measure.

Within Any Contraints

The main constraint is normally that of **time**. There should be a defined time limit or deadline as a part of **all** objectives.

Other constraints may include:

- resources,
- restrictions in authority,
- requirements by others,
- other people's competence.

Achievable

The objectives need to be achievable, attainable or accomplishable, otherwise we might get discouraged if we are constantly striving without success. We must feel that we are able to get the job done in the time available.

Challenging

If, however, the objectives are not challenging enough we will not be motivated to achieve them. They need to be challenging, without causing too much stress. How demanding, exacting or rigorous they are made is a matter of personal choice within the context of other events in the school. Leaders need to have a vision for the future of their school, therefore the evaluation and its objectives need to be innovatory. We need to look at new, different, varied aspects of the the school and the objectives of the evaluation need to reflect this. There should be a freshness, an enthusiasm, a looking forward to taking part and to finding out the results about the evaluation.

There needs to be a **balance** between the two elements of Achievable and Challenging.

FEW in number

The objectives of the evaluation should be minimised. One, two or three main objectives is good. Four or five is acceptable. More than five is too many.

Flexible

The objectives need to be flexible and adaptable within the current changing circumstances in schools, but not too flexible. If everything is constantly on the move we will lose direction.

Easily

The objectives should be easily and quickly **read.** They should be brief and coherent as possible. This does not mean, however, that they are necessarily easily **written** for this is often a difficult and time consuming activity.

Written

The objectives do need to be written and recorded. Firstly so that everybody knows what has been agreed, but secondly because the process of writing down and agreeing the objectives helps to clarify what is being planned for all concerned. The objectives should not be engraved in stone: bearing in mind the need for **balance** as the keynote.

Once again there needs to be a balance between the two elements of Flexible and Written:

OI! Do It Now

Do it **now!** Do not procrastinate. Setting the objectives for an evaluation is not an easy activity, but it is a necessary one and should not be delayed.

The final pair of aspects where there needs to be a balance is that between the needs of the Organisation and that of the Individual.

Organisational

The objectives of the evaluation need to be consistent with the goals of the school as a whole. They should be seen to be helping to achieve those goals by the completion of the evaluation in question. Thus the evaluation should not be isolated from what is happening elsewhere in the school. There should be clear links between the School Development Plan (SDP) and Departmental Plans. Organisational objectives should be public not private, that is they should be known to all those concerned.

Individual
The individuals involved in the evaluation should participate in setting the objectives for the evaluation if there is to be 'ownership' of the whole process. This is especially so for the outcomes of the evaluation and any consequent actions necessary. There may be a need for a balance between the 'personal' objectives and the 'professional' objectives of the individual and perhaps also a link with appraisal or development interviews. These objectives may be private and confidential to the individual contrasting with the public nature of organisational objectives.

If the above headings have been borne in mind then hopefully the objectives will be shared by all. Have they been communicated to all those who need or ought to know such as teachers, parents, governors, the LEA? Who is responsible for communicating the decision to evaluate?

WHO are the people who want the evaluation to be carried out? What are their reasons for this? Who wants the information the evaluation will provide? What are their reasons for this? On whose initiative will the evaluation take place? An even larger question is 'Is there agreement about the purpose? What is needed to get this agreement?' The micro-political questions concerning the people involved and their reasons, both declared and undeclared, are all too often ignored or not given enough consideration. They are fundamental questions, however, which need to be addressed and, even more importantly, have decisions made about them.

FOCUS AND EMPHASIS

It cannot be emphasised too much that it is important to ask what is the focus and emphasis of the evaluation? Focus on *what* information is required? Is the evaluation concerned with the whole school, a part of the whole school or an individual? The answer to this question would seem to be basic to the evaluation. The attitudes of those concerned will be very different if the evaluation is personal to the individual or to the individual as a part of a group.

Is the evaluation concerned with the teacher or the pupils? Perhaps an obvious question, but the issue is whether the evaluation is concerned with the pupils' learning and how successful or otherwise this has been, or is it concerned with the work that the teacher is doing and the delivery to the pupil? Sometimes it is almost impossible to separate the two things and this must be recognised.

Is the evaluation concerned with curriculum or management? Is the evaluation about the curriculum, is it about the management of the curriculum or is it solely concerned with management of the school? Once again these may be inextricably entwined or it may be possible to isolate that aspect which is to be evaluated.

Is the evaluation classroom based? Is the evaluation concerned only with what the teacher does in the classroom, or is it concerned with matters outside the learning environment?

The answers to these questions will determine the methods and processes which are to be used.

Many evaluations are much too vague and imprecise. Try to make *your* evaluation as focused as possible on one area of the school. It may be better to *in*clude additional items at a later stage, if that is necessary, rather than try to *ex*clude items because you have made the original focus too wide. Having focused on the precise detail, what is to be the emphasis? Is it to be on the inputs such as LMS, staff, resources, planning? Is it to be on the outputs like the children's learning or the number of children at level 3? Or is it to be on the processes, teaching and helping children to learn? Is it to be on the people or the product? Are all the teachers to be involved, or just individuals or groups? The decisions made at this stage should be recorded as suggested previously.

CRITERIA FOR JUDGEMENT

When criteria for judgement are being considered, we are concerned with the people involved in the evaluation and their attitudes to the criteria involved. Who will decide on the criteria? What are the nature and sources to be used for these criteria? Is there a place or a need for alternative criteria? How acceptable will they be to those involved? Will these criteria judge the worth of the aspects of the school to be studied? Will they measure the effectiveness of the school or whatever is being evaluated? The evaluation may or may not be imposed, by the governors, LEA, industry or Central Government. Decisions concerning criteria are often best made by the whole staff, and whoever else may be involved, working together to produce criteria which are acceptable to all concerned in the evaluation process itself.

VOLUNTARY OR IMPOSED

The voluntary or imposed element of evaluation will be considered at some length both here and in the section on three approaches to evaluation. **Is the evaluation voluntary or is it imposed**? The answer to this question concerns freedom. It is not only about whether to start the evaluation in the first place, but also as to whether it can be stopped at any stage and who has control over these decisions. These answers can influence the evaluation to a greater or lesser extent. It is linked to the questions asked earlier concerning initiative, as the imposition of an evaluation could cause much anxiety and resentment and hamper the whole evaluation process. It may be possible to 'sell' the idea of evaluation, in which case timing and 'readiness' may be issues. On the other hand, these issues may not need to be considered even if the evaluation has been imposed on those taking part, as long as the inherent problems are recognised. The main point would seem to be, **do those taking part think it is worthwhile**?

Is the evaluation developmental to those involved or is it more concerned with accountability? The answer to this, whether individual, group or whole school, is not only about the product of the evaluation, and the process, but is even more concerned with implementation and how to use the evaluation once it has been completed.

INTERNAL OR EXTERNAL

Is the evaluation internal or external to the educational establishment? This question would seem to be one of the first which needs to be addressed as the answer will affect the whole process, in particular the attitude of those concerned. If the evaluation is internal to the educational institution those concerned will normally see some purpose to it and may be more open in their comments. If the evaluation is external to the institution they may be more guarded in any comments which are made, in particular, any written evaluations. A potential area of major conflict may well arise if there are any misunderstandings as to whether the evaluation is internal or external to the institution. This is particularly so if those concerned treat the evaluation as internal and, at a later date, discover that others involved use the information gained outside the institution. The key here would seem to be one of *perceptions.* Some issues which might need consideration are the following:

- Are the governors internal or external to the school?
- How has their role changed since the 1988 Education Act?
- What are the perceptions of those concerned in the evaluation?

THREE APPROACHES TO EVALUATION

There now follow three approaches to evaluation in order to assist the reader to categorise the different types of relationships that exist within evaluation. The first two diagrams and their explanation are taken from Hughes, Ribbins and Thomas *Managing Education: The System and the Institution.*

CONDUCT WITHIN EVALUATION RELATIONSHIPS

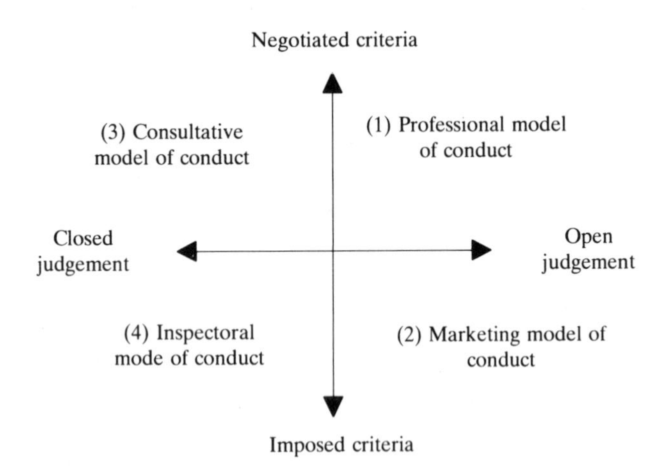

The diagram shows two crossing continua, these are:

Criteria continuum

Negotiated ◀————▶ Imposed

setting own or negotiated criteria — *criteria may not match desired objectives*

At one extreme the criteria for the evaluation are totally set by those who are conducting the evaluation and are likely to match the desired objectives or there is a large measure of negotiation. At the opposite end of the continuum, the criteria are imposed where they may not match the desired objectives. Hence, they are a potential cause of conflict.

Judgement continuum

Closed Judgement ◀——————▶	Open Judgement
those being evaluated have no part in preparing final evaluative statement	*those being evaluated do have a part in preparing evaluative statement*

On the judgement continuum an open judgement is one in which those being evaluated do have a part in preparing the final evaluative statement whereas at the opposite extreme, a closed judgement, they do not.

This produces four segments which are as follows:

1. **Professional conduct**
   In this segment, those being evaluated are able to set or negotiate the criteria and also to have a part in preparing the final evaluative statement. This sector gives the most freedom. An example of this is teachers' self-evaluation.

2. **Marketing model of conduct**
   In this segment, those being evaluated are not able to set or negotiate the criteria, but do have a part in preparing the final evaluative statement. An example of this is schools having to publish their exam. results, but being able to decide the form of that presentation.

3. **Consultative model of conduct**
   In this segment, those being evaluated are able to set or negotiate the criteria, but not the final judgement. An example of this might be LEA advisers working in a school.

4. **Inspectoral model of conduct**
   In this segment, those being evaluated have the criteria imposed, and do not have any part in preparing the final evaluative

statement. An example of this might be an OFSTED inspection with its subsequent report which is made public.

This approach is useful particularly when looking at segments 3 and 4. There may, or may not, have been a change in role of the LEA advisers from segment 3 to 4, that is from an advisory to an inspectoral role. This should not cause any conflict as long as everybody concerned is aware of the change. There is, however, potential for conflict if we think we are in segment 3, consultative model of conduct, and the adviser thinks he or she is in segment 4, inspectoral model of conduct. The approach and the diagram assist our thinking as we realise it is not a change in judgement, but a change in one of the criteria being used for the evaluation.

RELATIONSHIPS IN EVALUATION

Authority / By whom	Autonomy	Control	Authority / For whom
Internal	(1) Personal evaluation	(3) Internal assessment	Internal
	(2) Presentational review	(4) Public audit	External
External	(5) Consultancy	(7) Advice	Internal
	(6) Research	(8) Inspection	External

This diagram attempts to show the relationships which can exist between the evaluators and those who are evaluated within **three parameters** of authority:

Autonomy is where the evaluators and evaluated are free to enter or leave the process as they wish.

Control is where the evaluated are obliged to accept the evaluative activity of others upon them because these people control certain sanctions or rewards which are needed by the evaluated and who are thus controlled.

Authority:

By whom the evaluation is done is on the left of the diagram. This is subdivided into internal and external. **For whom** the evaluation is done is on the right of the diagram and once more includes the division into internal and external.

These three parameters combine to form eight possible sets of relationships. These are considered briefly in turn, with examples, below.

1. **Personal evaluation** is where the evaluation is a voluntary activity and carried out by the evaluator. An example of this might be a teacher evaluating her own work for herself, or a group of teachers evaluating their own work for themselves. This is the sort of activity in which teachers wishing to improve their work would engage privately.

2. **Presentational review** is a voluntary activity by the teacher, which may have been carried out by the teacher or another person in the institution, but in this instance the immediate outcome of the evaluation is for those other than the teacher concerned. An example of this might be a teacher wanting further resources inviting the Head into her classroom to see not only what is being done at present, but what could be done with increased resources. The evaluation has been entered into freely by the teacher, the evaluation is internal to the school, but the Head is external to the teacher being evaluated.

3. In **Internal assessment** the choice element is absent as in the case where the underlying ideology is 'managerial', and those in authority have the right and obligation to monitor and judge the work of subordinates. An example of this might be where the curriculum leader visits a teacher in the classroom so that they, together, can subsequently determine the staff development needs of the teacher. Another case is a teacher submitting a scheme of work for the approval of the Head. In both of these cases the evaluation is carried out internally to the school, but there is an element of control involved and the teacher has no choice about this.

4. The main difference between **Public audit** and earlier relationships is that the results of the evaluation are principally for somebody other than those being evaluated. Some examples of this might be the Head assessing several teachers before recommending to the governors his or her choice for an internal promotion. An LEA self-assessment scheme might also come under this heading, particularly if the governors or the LEA are seen as external to the school.

5. In the **Consultancy** relationship the evaluated teacher enters into a relationship voluntarily with an external evaluator, but the result is for internal use. This is a relatively unusual relationship for the individual teacher, but is becoming more common at whole school level.

6. **Research** by academics is a good instance of this relationship. It is entered into voluntarily by the school, but researchers are external to the school and the results are for an external audience as they are often published in a book or other journal.

7. In the **Advice** relationship the evaluator is external to the school, there is an element of control, but the purpose of the evaluation is for those being evaluated. The LEA adviser visiting the school where the results of the evaluation are for internal use or the LEA self-assessment scheme are both cases of the advice relationship if the results are for internal use, especially if the governors are seen as internal to the school.

8. An OFSTED **Inspection** would fall into this category as OFSTED inspectors are external to the institution, there is an element of control and the results are published publicly. It could be argued that the role of LEA inspectors falls in this segment as opposed to LEA advisers. Certainly their role may be changing in this way.

The main use of the 'Relationships in Evaluation' diagram is that it helps to categorise the different kinds of relationships and highlights the fact that any tensions or conflicts which arise often do so because of the **perceptions** of those involved. This is particularly so if those involved did not see themselves within the same segment, but in different ones. An instance of this is teacher appraisal. Which segment do you think that it should be in? Is this perception shared by those who are also involved within the school?

STAKE'S DIMENSIONS FOR CLASSIFYING EVALUATION DESIGNS

The third approach to evaluation is Stake's dimensions for classifying evaluation designs. This is particularly useful as many of the terms which are in current parlance are used, but are combined in a series of continua which are shown below. In order to understand the first of these continua Stake suggests the example of a cook making some soup for guests. When the cook tastes the soup (the left hand side of the continuum) it might be done in order to adjust the seasoning by adding more salt and pepper and is therefore developmental and diagnostic as it can change the result before the end of the process. When the guests taste the soup (the right hand side of the continuum) it is at the end of the cooking process and is therefore more evaluative. The key to this evaluation process is not so much *when* as *why*. What is the information for? The dimensions are as follows and also include some additional notes from Stake's work in order to help clarify each dimension.

FORMATIVE	◄——►	**SUMMATIVE**
Developmental		At the end
Diagnostic		Evaluative
Continuous assessment		Examinations
Professional development		Accountability
INFORMAL	◄——►	**FORMAL**
Personal		Impersonal
Internal		External
		Accurate, valid, credible
CASE PARTICULAR	◄——►	**GENERALISATION**
Fixed ultimate target		Representative of others
Worth of particular programme		Worth of general approach
PROCESS	◄——►	**PRODUCT**
Transactions		Outcomes
Intrinsic value		Payoff value
DESCRIPTIVE	◄——►	**JUDGEMENTAL**
RESPONSIVE	◄——►	**PREORDINATE**
Subjective		Objective
No prior expectations		Prior expectations

METHODS

The questions about methods once again concern people as well as techniques. Is it to be a 'one off' evaluation? Is it to be repeated or is it to be part of a planned programme? What are the appropriate methods? Direct observation, questionnaires, interviews, examination of documents, for example, could all be used, but which is the most appropriate for the evaluation in question? Are these appropriate methods for the time available? A number of practical methods will be given in the following chapters of this book which may help readers to make the right choice for their school. How to gather the information required raises issues of knowledge and acceptability as well as appropriateness, in addition to linking this with the purpose and focus of the evaluation. Have those people making the evaluation got the knowledge and experience of the techniques needed? If not, what do they need to do to acquire this knowledge? If it is decided to use direct observation, for example, is this acceptable to those being evaluated? How detailed are the methods going to be? What evaluative judgements are going to be made? Are these acceptable? Is the evaluation confined to teachers, or do other staff in the school contribute? Do pupils, parents, governors, LEA advisers or inspectors have a part to play? Is there a place for external consultants or observers? Issues here might be seen as questions concerning who is internal and external to the school as mentioned earlier in the chapter. The decisions to be made are rarely simple and are more often than not concerning people and their feelings as much as techniques.

STYLES OF EVALUATION

Six styles, or models, of overlapping evaluation have been identified by Lawton in *The Politics of the School Curriculum* and can be briefly explained:

- The agricultural-botanical research style
- The research and development style
- The anthropological style
- The briefing the decision-makers style
- The teacher as a researcher style
- The case-study style

THE AGRICULTURAL-BOTANICAL RESEARCH STYLE

In this style of evaluation, which is linked with agricultural-botanical research, everything is quantitatively measured. For example the height of a plant is measured, the amount of water added is measured, the amount of fertiliser added is measured and after a measured time the height of the plant is remeasured. It may be that 'controls' involving similar plants are introduced where the light is controlled, or different amounts of water and fertiliser added. In this style of evaluation each input and output is measured as carefully as possible.

THE RESEARCH AND DEVELOPMENT STYLE

This is sometimes called the industrial or factory model as it suggests a research and development department which takes samples from the items being manufactured which are then measured quantitatively. The information thus gained is fed back into the system with any of the necessary changes having been made.

These first two styles depend on quantifiable results from tests. When used in educational settings they are often based on behavioural objectives and measurements, and therefore take an impoverished view of educational experience. Nevertheless these styles may be applied to education where testing can be used and where results of tests are seen to be important.

THE ANTHROPOLOGICAL STYLE

This style is exactly the opposite from the previous two. In this style the evaluator becomes a part of what is being evaluated and tries to analyse and interpret what is seen from the inside. This style offers a qualitative account of events where the primary concern is with description and interpretation rather than with measurement and prediction.

These three styles of evaluation all tend to take simplistic views of a complex process as they only use one form of measurement. The next three mix both qualitative and quantitative methods.

THE BRIEFING THE DECISION-MAKERS' STYLE

In the three variations of this style the evaluator seeks to make explicit his or her political stance, hence the reason this is sometimes called the political style of evaluation. The attempt is thus to clarify areas of interpretive uncertainty and is based on the work of MacDonald in Tawney (Ed.) *Curriculum Evaluation Today*.

1. **The bureaucratic evaluator** accepts the values of the bureaucrats who hire him and simply aims to leave behind a satisfied client. For example, if as an evaluator, I know you wish to find out that children read poorly then I devise a test to show this. If I know that you wish to find out that children read well then I devise a test to show this. The aim, remember, is to leave behind a satisfied client. It might be seen that many of those who devise tests for LEA and national use fall into this category.
2. **The autocratic evaluator** sticks to particular educational principles and insists that his or her advice is taken in devising and interpreting the evaluation. By choosing the right autocratic evaluator to examine an area, administrators can effectively get what they want without taking the ultimate decisions. It might be seen that the repeated change of those involved with certain National Curriculum areas, until an 'acceptable' result was obtained, falls into this category.
3. **The democratic evaluator** recognises that there is no agreement about fundamental educational issues and tries to be an 'honest broker', presenting data without making any recommendations – at least initially. The interpretations of the data are established as a result of negotiation between the evaluators and those who employ them. The question that might be asked here is, 'Can the truth be negotiated?'

THE TEACHER AS A RESEARCHER STYLE

This is an evaluation style where the teacher both develops and evaluates whatever is under observation, for example what is happening in the classroom. The problem with this style is that it is difficult to be entirely objective about something in which you, personally, are involved. The teacher may, therefore, seek to be more objective by using 'triangulation'. This is a process where the teacher monitors by comparing his or her account of what has happened with that of an observer or a pupil in order to obtain a view for comparison.

THE CASE-STUDY STYLE

In this style, the objective is to study one specific example in depth, in order to portray the 'whole' scene. To achieve this objective, a mixed mode strategy including a variety of techniques, is used, such as measurements, questionnaires, interviews, in an attempt to obtain as many contrasting views of the same objective and hence 'the truth'.

ORGANISATION AND PLANNING

The questions and subsequent decisions about organisation and planning are, perhaps, less to do with people's feelings. So, how will the programme be organised? What are the constraints? Who will undertake the evaluation?

How will the information be gathered and who will gather it? This can be a major question and an area of potential conflict, particularly if it is also linked with the first of the questions, is the evaluation internal or external to the institution? On the other hand it may not be a political question at all, but rather an organisational one, and concerned with the practicalities and details of information gathering.

Planning in education is as much concerned with what is possible as with what is desirable. It is necessary to emphasise the importance of balance in schools between a time-consuming systematic approach to planning and no planning at all. It may be that a list is all that is needed, but it is more likely that an **ACTION PLAN** which is more systematic will be appropriate. This should include:

WHO should do **WHAT** by **WHEN**

that is:

A NAMED PERSON(S)	carrying out a **SPECIFIC ACTIVITY**	with a **TIME** for completion

If the evaluation is complex, planning techniques such as the following may be required:

- **Key Events Planning** which is a list of events with the date (or time) when each event is planned to occur.
- **Milestone Planning** where dates are listed at fixed intervals and required outcomes for each date are stated.
- **Bar chart of Gantt Chart Planning** where identical activities are shown as bars against a timescale. The length of the bar represents the expected duration of the activity. The process requires careful identification of each stage of the process and an accurate estimation of the time involved.

These techniques are potentially helpful in:

- specifying objectives
- identifying activities
- prioritising activities
- establishing relationships between activities
- negotiating time and resources.

They do, however, require expertise, are not always readily understandable and there is a danger of 'overkill'. It is worth re-stating that planning is a necessary managerial activity that is often neglected.

RESOURCES

This leads to questions about resources. These can be viewed *positively* and need not be considered necessarily as negative. Evaluation does require resources, the main one being time. Those involved must recognise this and plan not only for the resources which are needed, but also allow for the constraints which a lack of resources imposes. What resources are needed? This may be in the form of equipment, back-up facilities, paper for the reports, duplicating and other reprographic equipment, typewriters or wordprocessors and perhaps more important when considering resources, their availability when they are needed. What equipment could save time, the greatest of all the resources which are likely to be needed? It may be interesting to add up the resources, including time, at the *end* of the whole evaluation and to compare them with those costs that were anticipated at the beginning.

TIME

The problems of time, however, and the attitudes to it, may be strongly linked to the points which were being made about the voluntary nature or imposition of evaluation. Teachers never seem to have enough time and thus the evaluation must be seen by those concerned to be worthwhile if they are to give their time to it. What time will be available? Is this time available already or does it need to be 'created'? If so, how? Is this realistic? Can the information required be gathered in the time available? The time schedule and keeping to it need to be considered as a part of the planning. In general terms, too little time seems to be allowed, not only for collection of data, but also for reflection and thought about what to do with the information once it has been gathered.

REPORTING

In reporting the evaluation, what form will it take? Will it be verbal, written, multi-media? Who will actually compile and make the report? Who is the report for and what is the intended audience (note the links here with the previous chapter)? Will it include *all* the findings? Does there need to be a balance between description and evaluation data and opinion? How much analysis and reflection is needed? Are there references to teacher performance? Are individuals named, or is it anonymous? Is there reference to children and their performance or outcomes? Is this acceptable to all concerned? Once again the micro-politics of the situation need to be considered. Reporting is strongly linked to the next item.

CONTROL AND AVAILABILITY OF THE INFORMATION

The type of questions on control and availability of the information are those about the ownership of the information and who has control. Who has the decision about the final form of the report? What about confidentiality and openness? Will the report be seen by all those involved, or only some of them? Is their agreement needed for the report as a whole, or just parts of it pre-'publication'? What are the procedures and who decides what they are? Is this acceptable to all concerned? To whom will the findings of the evaluation be available? Who will see that they do, in fact, receive it? Perhaps the key here is the need for tact and consideration.

EFFECTIVENESS OF THE EXERCISE (EVALUATION OF THE EVALUATION)

What about the effectiveness of the exercise (evaluation of the evaluation)? If evaluation is to be effective then it in turn will need to be evaluated. It is an area which is often excluded on the grounds of lack of time, and also that this part of the evaluation normally comes at the end when enthusiasm has started to wane. Harlen and Elliott in McCormick (Ed.) *Calling Education to Account* give some questions for reviewing (evaluating) evaluations which are:

- Did the evaluation serve to inform the decisions or judgements for which it was originally intended?
- What decisions have been taken as a consequence of the evaluation?
- Was the evaluation task interpreted and carried through consistently as intended?
- Was the information which was gathered appropriate to the purpose of the evaluation?
- What steps were taken to allow for bias, unrepresentativeness, and low reliability in the information gathered?
- Were the actual evaluators in the best position to carry out the evaluation?
- Were the methods used appropriate to the kind of information which was required?
- Were the methods systematic and explicit?
- Did those involved in supplying the information approve of the methods used for collecting it?
- Was there sufficient time allowed in the evaluation for the necessary data to be collected?
- Was the evaluation carried out at the best time to serve its purpose?
- What were the side effects, positive and negative, of the evaluation process?
- Were satisfactory procedures used to protect the interests of those who supplied information?

- Were the criteria by which judgement or decisions were made appropriately drawn and explicitly stated?
- Was the evaluation reported in a way which communicated effectively with the intended audience?
- What reactions did the report provoke in the participants and the decision-makers?

These questions could be applied to some examples of completed evaluations, as a useful planning exercise and the further question, 'If not why not?' used as a necessary follow up to initial answers. This question may bring to light issues which should be considered not just after an evaluation is carried out, but also *before.*

APPLICATION AND USE OF THE EVALUATION

The final, and perhaps most important question to be asked is, **so what**? What is the application and use of the evaluation having completed it? What action has resulted? What changes have been made in the school? Has there been evidence of fresh or revitalised thinking? Are there procedures set up beforehand to ensure the evaluation *will* have some effect or will the evaluation merely gather dust on a shelf? This brings us back to the point about the purpose of the evaluation in the first place.

HUMAN FACTORS OF EVALUATION

The 'human' factors of evaluation are considered as a conclusion to this chapter which overviews the practical aspects of evaluation. These positive factors are:

- worthwhile
- high priority
- timing
- inform practice
- integral
- involvement
- ownership.

WORTHWHILE

The first and most important of these is that the teachers and any others involved with the evaluation should regard it as worthwhile. Normally this means for primary school teachers that it should provide some sort of benefit to the children in the classroom, if not immediately, then at some foreseeable time in the future. It should also be seen to revitalise the school and, hopefully, to release energy for its further development. The aim is to clear the mind and to improve understanding of what the school is trying to achieve and is achieving and to maintain morale.

HIGH PRIORITY

If the evaluation is seen as worthwhile then it must have a high priority for the whole school. This means that everybody should know that it is a high priority; teachers, children, parents, governors and anybody else involved. It may also mean that other activities may have to be reduced, not only in terms of effort, but also of time.

TIMING

Timing of this priority can be problematic, as there are so many priorities at the present time that it is difficult, if not impossible, to have just one priority. Nevertheless, not everything can be top priority, and the fitting together is a planned order and the timing of different evaluations and initiatives is the job of the Head and other senior staff.

INFORM PRACTICE

Evaluation should inform practice. It is only by evaluating what is being done now and what has been done in the past that the future can be planned with confidence. This is true not only for individuals, but also for groups and indeed the whole school. It allows for all the differing views and perceptions to come together to make a whole. It is by improving on what is being done well and also by putting right the things which are not going so well that a better provision is made for the children who are at the heart of primary education.

INTEGRAL

If evaluation is to inform practice then it must be an integral part of what happens in the school. Evaluation should be seen as a positive, encouraging aspect of the work that is being done. Most of the time positive factors will come out of evaluation. It will thus be uplifting and encouraging to repeat the process, rather than being a threatening or negative activity.

INVOLVEMENT

It is important that **ALL** the teachers are involved in **ALL** the steps of an evaluation. That is in the planning, execution and review of the evaluation and not just the execution part. Holly in his chapter 'Making it Count: Evaluation for the Developing Primary School' in Southworth's book *Readings in Primary School Management*, says that self-evaluation in the primary school is more likely to be internal as opposed to external evaluation. It is done

- **by** the members of staff—with appropriate support
- **for** the members of staff
- **for** and **with** the participant practitioners

it is not a case of the work being done

- **to** or **at** these same participants.

OWNERSHIP

In this way, ownership of the evaluation and its findings will be created. This will be encouraged if confidentiality is respected and if each stage is seen as being acceptable to all those concerned. These aspects of caring for the human side of evaluation do take a little extra time by those who are managing the process, but will bear fruit and make it even more worthwhile.

These positive aspects of evaluation have been emphasised whilst it is recognised that some teachers see evaluation as a negative process. This is probably because for them evaluation is seen as irrelevant and not worthwhile. It has a low priority for the teacher and the school, the timing is poor and it does not inform practice. It is seen as an additional piece of work, yet another thing that has to be done and is probably looking at weaknesses. It is something which is done *to* you rather than your being involved and of which you have no ownership.

In this chapter some of the basic principles of evaluation have been considered in order to help those involved in an evaluation to focus their own views and perceptions. It has also attempted to give the reader some tools to assist in seeing their own evaluation within a wider context of evaluation in general and the perceptions which others may have.

ACTIVITIES

Some of the questions which have been asked in this chapter are now presented in a form which may make them easier to use as activities.

It is essential for anybody attempting any of these activities that an actual example of an evaluation is considered; either one which has recently been completed or one which is identified as an area or issue which might benefit from an exercise in evaluation in your school in the future. The activities will not work as well if evaluation in general terms is considered.

THE PURPOSE OF THE EVALUATION

What is the purpose of the evaluation?

What events have caused the evaluation to be needed?

Why are we carrying out the evaluation?

How will we know when it has been completed?

What are the measurable objectives of the evaluation?

Are these objectives shared by all?

Have they been communicated to all teachers, parents, governors, the LEA?

To whom is it necessary to communicate the decision to evaluate?

THE OBJECTIVES OF THE EVALUATION

Objectives should be:

SMART
- Specific
- Measurable
- Attainable
- Realistic
- Time constrained

MAC FEW OI!
- Measurable with Any Constraints
- Achievable
- Challenging

FEW in number
- Flexible
- Easily
- Written

OI! Do it now!
- Organisation
- Individual

What are the objectives of your evaluation?

What needs to be done for these objectives to be shared by all involved in the evaluation?

To whom is it necessary to communicate these objectives?

WHO WANTS THE EVALUATION?

Who wants the evaluation to be carried out?

What are their reasons for this?

Who wants the information the evaluation will provide?

What are their reasons for this?

On whose initiative will the evaluation take place?

Is there agreement about the purpose?

What is needed to get this agreement?

THE BASIC QUESTIONS

The following questions need to be considered in order to establish the focus of the evaluation.

Is the evaluation internal or external to the educational establishment?

Is the evaluation concerned with the whole school, a part of the whole school or an individual?

Is the evaluation developmental to those involved or is it more concerned with accountability?

Is the evaluation voluntary or is it imposed?

How will the information be gathered and who will gather it?

Who is the evaluation for and how will it be presented?

What is to be done with the evaluation?

Is the evaluation concerned with the teacher or the pupils?

Is the evaluation concerned with curriculum or management?

Is the evaluation classroom based?

THE FOCUS AND EMPHASIS OF THE EVALUATION

What is the focus of the evaluation?

Which aspects of school life are to be evaluated?
(curriculum areas, teaching, learning, administration, etc.)

What INFORMATION is required?

What is to be the EMPHASIS?

Is it to be on the INPUTS?
(such as LMS, staff, resources, planning)

Is it to be on the OUTPUTS?
(like the children's learning or the number of children at level 3)

Is it to be on the PROCESSES?
(teaching and helping children to learn)

Is it to be on the PEOPLE or the PRODUCT?

Are all the teachers to be involved, or just individuals or groups?

CRITERIA FOR JUDGEMENT OF THE EVALUATION

Who will decide on the criteria?

What is the nature of these criteria?

What sources are to be used for these criteria?

Is there a place or a need for alternative criteria?

How acceptable are they to those involved?

Will these criteria judge the worth of the aspects of the school to be studied?

Will they measure the effectiveness of the school or whatever is being evaluated?

Make a list of the criteria to be used in the evaluation.

Decisions concerning criteria are often best made by the whole staff working together to produce their own criteria which are acceptable to all concerned.

CONDUCT WITHIN EVALUATION RELATIONSHIPS

Place your evaluation on each of the two continua

Criteria continuum

Negotiated ◄——————► Imposed
setting own or negotiated criteria — *criteria may not match desired objectives*

Judgement continuum

Closed Judgement ◄——————► Open Judgement
those being evaluated have no part in preparing final evaluative statement — *those being evaluated do have a part in preparing final evaluative statement*

Now place the evaluation on this diagram in the correct segment.

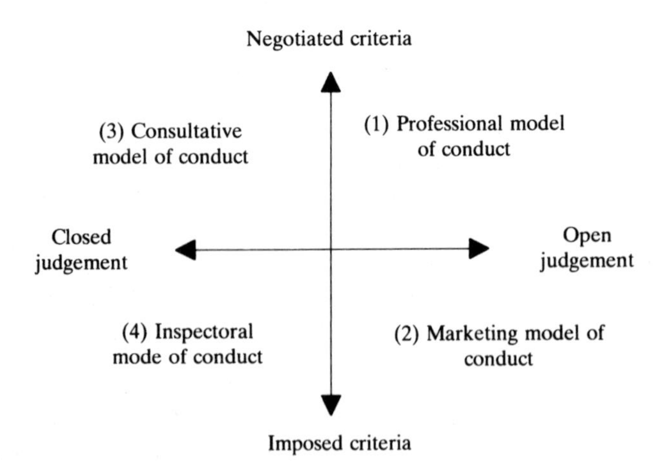

Finally, check your perceptions with somebody else involved with the evaluation to see if they put it in the same segment. If they do not, why not?

RELATIONSHIPS IN EVALUATION

Firstly, decide on the relationships which exist between the evaluators and those who are evaluated within the three parameters.

Autonomy/control
Have the persons being evaluated autonomy or are they controlled?

By whom is the evaluation being done?
Internal or external?

For whom is the evaluation being done?
Internal or external?

These three parameters combine to form eight possible sets of relationships. Place your evaluation on this diagram in the correct segment.

Authority / By whom	Autonomy	Control	Authority / For whom
Internal	(1) Personal evaluation	(3) Internal assessment	Internal
	(2) Presentational review	(4) Public audit	External
External	(5) Consultancy	(7) Advice	Internal
	(6) Research	(8) Inspection	External

Finally, check your perceptions with somebody else involved with the evaluation to see if they put it in the same segment. If they do not, why not?

STAKE'S DIMENSIONS

Where would you put your evaluation on each of these continua?

FORMATIVE	◀——▶	**SUMMATIVE**
Developmental		At the end
Diagnostic		Evaluative
INFORMAL	◀——▶	**FORMAL**
Personal		Impersonal
Internal		External
CASE PARTICULAR	◀——▶	**GENERALISATION**
Fixed ultimate target		Representative of others
Worth of particular programme		Worth of general approach
PROCESS	◀——▶	**PRODUCT**
Transactions		Outcomes
Intrinsic value		Payoff value
DESCRIPTIVE	◀——▶	**JUDGEMENTAL**
RESPONSIVE	◀——▶	**PREORDINATE**
Subjective		Objective
No prior expectations		Prior expectations
HOLISTIC	◀——▶	**ANALYTIC**
Whole		Key characteristics
Case study		
INTERNAL	◀——▶	**EXTERNAL**
Insiders		Outsiders

METHODS

Is it to be a ‘one off’ evaluation?

Is it to be repeated?

Is it part of a planned programme?

What are the appropriate methods for the evaluation?

Are these acceptable to those being evaluated?

Have those people making the evaluation got the knowledge and experience of the techniques needed?

If not, what do they need to do to acquire this knowledge?

How detailed are the methods going to be?

What evaluative judgements are going to be made?

Are these acceptable?

Is the evaluation confined to teachers?

Do other staff in the school contribute to the evaluation?

Do pupils, parents, governors, LEA advisers or inspectors have a part to play?

Is there a place for external consultants or observers?

STYLES OF EVALUATION

Which of these six styles, or models, of evaluation may be identified as being appropriate for your evaluation?

The agricultural-botanical research style

The research and development style

The anthropological style

The briefing the decision-makers style

The teacher as a researcher style

The case-study style.

THE ORGANISATION AND PLANNING OF THE EVALUATION

How will the programme be organised?

What are the constraints?

Who will undertake the evaluation? (Put the names of the people involved.)

ACTION PLAN

WHO should do **WHAT** by **WHEN**

A NAMED PERSON(S)	carrying out a **SPECIFIC ACTIVITY**	with a **TIME** for completion

RESOURCES FOR THE EVALUATION

What **resources** are needed?

Are these available when they are needed?

What equipment could save time?

What **time** is needed for the evaluation?

Is this time available already or does it need to be 'created'?

If so, how?

Is this realistic?

Can the information required be gathered in the time available?

REPORTING THE EVALUATION

What form will the report of the evaluation take?
(Will it be verbal, written, multi-media?)

Who will actually compile and make the report?

Who is the report for and what is the intended audience?

Will the report include *all* the findings?

Does there need to be a balance between description and evaluation data and opinion?

How much analysis and reflection are needed?

Are there references to teacher performance?

Are individuals named, or is it anonymous?

Is there reference to children and their performance or outcomes?

Is this acceptable to all concerned?

CONTROL AND AVAILABILITY OF THE INFORMATION

Who has the decisions about the final form of the report?

What about confidentiality and openness?

Will the report be seen by all those involved, or only some of them?

Is their agreement needed for the report as a whole, or parts of it before 'publication'?

What are the procedures and who decides what they are?

Is this acceptable to all concerned?

To whom will the findings of the evaluation be available?

Who will see that they do, in fact, receive it?

EFFECTIVENESS OF THE EXERCISE (EVALUATION OF THE EVALUATION)

Harlen and Elliott in McCormick (Ed.) *Calling Education to Account* give some questions for reviewing evaluations which are:

Did the evaluation serve to inform the decisions or judgements for which it was originally intended?

What decisions have been taken as a consequence of the evaluation?

Was the evaluation task interpreted and carried through consistently as intended?

Was the information which was gathered appropriate to the purpose of the evaluation?

What steps were taken to allow for bias, unrepresentativeness, and low reliability in the information gathered?

Were the actual evaluators in the best position to carry out the evaluation?

Were the methods used appropriate to the kind of information which was required?

Were the methods systematic and explicit?

Did those involved in supplying the information approve of the methods used for collecting it?

Was there sufficient time allowed in the evaluation for the necessary data to be collected?

Was the evaluation carried out at the best time to serve its purpose?

What were the side effects, positive and negative, of the evaluation process?

Were satisfactory procedures used to protect the interests of those who supplied information?

Were the criteria, by which judgement or decisions were made, appropriately drawn and explicitly stated?

Was the evaluation reported in a way which communicated effectively with the intended audience?

What reactions did the report provoke in the participants and the decision-makers?

APPLICATION AND USE OF THE EVALUATION

What action has resulted from the evaluation?

What changes have been made in the school as a result of the evaluation?

Has there been evidence of fresh or revitalised thinking? If so, what?

Are there any procedures which could be set up beforehand to ensure the evaluation *will* have some effect?

How do the applications and use of the evaluation link to the expressed purposes of the evaluation in the first place?

2
Whole School Evaluation

This chapter will begin by the consideration of two areas:

- Accountability and development
- Constraints

The main body of the chapter will be a synopsis and comments on methods of evaluating the school as a whole, namely:

- A five stage guide
- SBR—School Based Review
- GRIDS—Guidelines for Review and Internal Development in Schools
- IMTEC/SDG—International Movements Towards Educational Change/School Development Guide
- DION—Diagnosing Individual and Organisational Needs
- The role of critical colleagues
- DIY—Do It Yourself method
- Additional methods
  LEA evaluation schemes
  The ILEA checklist
  Taking professional stock
  SWOT
  The use of OFSTED materials.

The chapter will conclude with some of the issues which may not have been considered already:

- Climate
- Relationships
- Small schools
- Improvement on the second cycle.

ACCOUNTABILITY AND DEVELOPMENT

There are perhaps two conflicting purposes for evaluation of performance. One is for **accountability**, to **prove quality**. The other is for **development**, to **improve quality**. There would seem to be two main extremes on this continuum: at one end, inspection-based and external, at the other one based on self-evaluation. A continuum model to include all these elements might give:

ACCOUNTABILITY ◄————► DEVELOPMENT
EXTERNAL ◄————► INTERNAL
INSPECTION-BASED ◄————► SELF-EVALUATION
TO PROVE QUALITY ◄————► TO IMPROVE QUALITY

It has been suggested that there has been a move towards the left hand end of this continuum during the 1980s. It could be argued that the converse is also true in that the greater involvement of parents and governors in evaluating practice in schools, as encouraged by the successive Education Acts of 1980, 1981, 1986 and finally the ERA in 1988, have all emphasised evaluation by those internal to the school. This depends on whether parents and governors are seen as internal or external to the school. There is also a danger that schools may be tempted to respond to externally imposed schemes by producing whatever is required without themselves using the data for review of professional practice in the school. Even if the activity does affect practice in positive ways, it may cease when the external demand fades. Different schools or even individual evaluations from the same school can be placed separately on the continuum. It might also be that evaluations made in the same school, but at different times, are placed differently.

It may be that accountability and development are not necessarily opposites on a continuum, but that there has to be a **balance** between development and accountability or even a bringing together and integration of the two.

THE RELATIONSHIP BETWEEN EVALUATION AND ACCOUNTABILITY

This will now be considered in some depth as the two can be and are seen by some as inextricably intertwined. It can be argued that the changes which have been introduced in education as a result of the Education Acts of the 1980s and in particular the 1988 ERA are a result of a perceived need for greater accountability. Three differing aspects of accountability are considered: the East Sussex Accountability Project, the Models of Accountability of Adelman & Alexander and finally on a more practical note, the approach advocated by Nuttall.

The **East Sussex Accountability Project** carried out by the University of Sussex in 1979 was a researched project which investigated various views on accountability. They did this by interviewing parents, teachers, local authority officers, governors and politicians. They suggest that accountability can have a positive as well as a negative aspect and it is a two-way process. They continue that it is possible to approach accountability as a process of mutual negotiation as opposed to the imposition of a solution.

The project identified three kinds of accountability:

- **Answerability** to one's clients, i.e. parents and pupils (moral accountability).
- **Responsibility** to oneself and one's colleagues (professional accountability).
- **Accountability** in the strict sense to one's employers or political masters (contractual accountability).

They suggest that accountability must meet two basic interconnecting demands which might be summarised as:

Maintenance procedures: preserving and enhancing general levels of performance.

Problem-solving: the detection and amelioration of individual points of weakness.

These elements of schools' accountability are summarised in a table which is taken from McCormick, R. (Ed.) *Calling Education to Account.*

The project suggests that all categories are dependent on context and that the demarcation line between them will vary from time to time and place to place. It would seem that these categories could be adapted and defined for an individual or school. The project

	Answerability (to parents)	**Responsibility** (to self and peers)	**Strict Accountability** (to LEA direct or via managers)
MAINTENANCE	1: —Regular communication on individual children's progress (via written reports etc.); —Accounts of overall policy (via prospectus etc.). Explanation of curricular aims and methods; —Reports on general standards of performance, academic and other (via open days, speech days etc.); —Encouragement of better parental awareness of school's activities and endeavours (via ready access to classrooms and staff, atmosphere of open enquiries and discussion).	3: —Domestic monitoring of standards; —Regular revew of staffing, curricula and teaching arrangements; —Promotion of good relationships with parents (via school social occasions etc.); —Promotion of good relationships with feeder and receiving (secondary) schools; —Promotion of good relationships with managers, advisers, and LEA as a whole.	5: —Observation of mandatory and constitutional procedures; —Meeting of centrally agreed specifications; —Openness to authorized visitation; —Readiness to justify curricular goals and methods and overall policies; —Readiness to account for pupil performance standards.
PROBLEM SOLVING	2. —Notification to all parents of complaints procedures; —Prompt acknowledgement and investigation of parental complaints, conformation of action taken; —Early disclosure to parents, where appropriate, of problems (i) relating to individual children (ii) involving wider issues	4: —Screening of individual children at risk (via internal reporting, pupil records, tests, etc.); —Provision of remedial help to children in need; —Awareness of incipient points of weakness; —Anticipation of potential crises.	6: —Reporting of unresolved external complaints and grievances; —Reporting of unresolved internal difficulties; —Development of effective means to deal with problems arising.

NB: The entries above are not intended to be comprehensive. They are meant only to indicate possible expectations or demands in each category. They should *not* be taken as indicating policies which are necessarily feasible, desirable or deserving of priority at the school level.

also looked at the LEA's accountability which has similar elements. Their final conclusion is that the time may come when accountability becomes a major influence on policy decisions and that it may encourage the critical review of existing policies and the identification of new initiatives. In 1979, these ideas were at the margin. In the 1990s, it might be thought, these ideas are a reality.

The location of *control* of the central evaluation decisions is related to the accountability relationship by Adelman & Alexander in *The Self-Evaluating Institution.* They suggest there are five 'ideal types' of accountability, which are:

- The Professional autonomy model
- The Managerial model
- The Consultative model
- The Mutual culpability model
- The Proletarian model.

The **Professional autonomy** model reflects the assumption that what goes on in a particular educational institution, course or classroom is the responsibility of each of the professionals concerned. It is suggested that the status as 'professional' is a guarantee of the integrity of such evaluation. The professional retains control over the key evaluation decisions, what to evaluate, how, to whom to disseminate findings and what action to take in the light of them. This is not properly a model for *institutional* self-evaluation since it is the opposite of the collective sense which is needed for this approach.

The **Managerial** model reflects the assumption that the individual is formally accountable to those who administer and control the course or institution to which he or she contributes and who allocates human and other resources to his or her work.

The **Consultative** model reflects the view that, as professionals, individuals in an institutional hierarchy have a right to be involved in discussions about their work, but that the form of such involvement and the control of evaluation decisions still rests with 'management'.

The **Mutual culpability** model reflects the view that all who participate directly in a particular educational activity have a legitimate interest in its quality and progress. Such quality and progress are the result of the particular contribution which each participating group or individual makes, and that, therefore, participants should be accountable to each other for their various contributions. Control of the evaluation decisions rests with the participants, and in organisational terms steps have to be taken to prevent the domination by one group.

The **Proletarian** model is the exact opposite of managerial accountability in that the accounting relationship is downwards from those given managerial responsibility to the 'workers'. At the same time, it is neither a 'professional autonomy model' (since it is collectivist rather than individualist) nor 'mutual culpability' (since the accountability is one-way only). This implies student and/or grass roots staff control.

On a more practical note, Nuttall, in *Accountability and Evaluation* in Open University Press E364 Block 1 Part C proposes that an accountability scheme should:

- be fair and perceived as fair by all the parties involved
- be capable of suggesting appropriate remedies
- yield an account that is intelligible to its intended audience(s)
- be methodologically sound
- be economic in its use of resources
- be an acceptable blend of centralised and delegated control.

It might be interesting for the reader to decide which of these models might be most appropriately applied to a particular evaluation in which they have been recently involved.

CONSTRAINTS

There are, however, constraints to school self-evaluation. Day, Johnston and Whitaker in their book *Managing Primary Schools: A Professional Development Approach* divided these into three:

- Practical factors—such as time, energy, skills and resources.
- Sociological factors—teachers operate within the norms of the school in which they work. These are often implicit.
- Psychological factors—change can be seen as threatening.

It is also worth mentioning that there may well be a difference between what people *say*, their intentions or aspirations, conscious or otherwise, and what they *do*, their practice in action.

Staff and students are most likely to participate in an evaluation which makes minimal demands on their time, and which will not expose their individual weaknesses to public scrutiny.

The view of many critics of self-evaluation based systems is that they are not sufficiently rigorous and systematic. It is suggested here that self-review, enhanced by co-operation with officers, governors and advisers, characterised by agreed agenda, by institutional ownership and responsibility for records and reports, is not a soft option. Far from it, it is argued, for interaction is much harder than any inspection systems. To reinforce the views put forward earlier, it is better to adopt a system of

- '**looking with**' rather than '**looking at**'

what is going on in schools and it is only by

- '**doing with**' rather than '**doing to**'

that there is likely to be an improvement in the quality of schooling which is to the benefit of the pupils in them.

To give those in schools some 'building blocks' with which to build school improvements, there now follows a number of methods to help achieve this.

A FIVE STAGE GUIDE

The stages are:

- Choose a method
- Plan
- Execute
- Evaluate
- Action.

CHOOSE A METHOD

Choose a method which is appropriate to your needs. It is important to consult and involve the staff in this, as it is only by doing so that it will be 'owned' by the school and the staff in it. It may be that you have chosen one of the methods such as the matrix method of

SBR or GRIDS or you may have adapted one of these or have a method of your own. The main point is that it is *your* method that *you* think is appropriate and that it is linked to a particular task at your school.

PLAN

Plan the procedure. It will be more effective if all those involved in the evaluation are a part of the planning procedure, especially if it utilises a systematic and self-conscious methodology. Some examples of plans were given in the previous chapter, some alternatives are given here. A plan should involve the following tasks:

- list the areas in which development is needed
- place the items in order of importance
- make a time/action plan
- work through the items planning an informal programme, or a formal programme.

An **informal programme** involves:

- defining objectives
- creating, seeking out, using opportunities as they occur to achieve objectives.

A **formal programme** involves:

- defining objectives
- listing people to involve, consult, inform
- identifying actions needed
- making a time/action plan
- planning evaluation.

An **effective plan** will be:

- explicit
- intelligible
- capable of accepting change
- capable of being monitored.

EXECUTE

It is also right and proper that the teachers should be involved in the planning stage as it is they who will have to execute the procedure. This will include both the process itself and the product. The **process** is valuable in itself particularly if it emphasises a clear perception and definition of process and role. There should be a heightened awareness of needs by all of those involved and also a perception of the 'whole' school needs by the individual. There should be more insight into strengths and weaknesses of the school and the individual. It is worthwhile to decide how the strengths can be built upon and the weaknesses minimised. Within the process the value and use of outside help should be understood and not underestimated.

The **product** may include some or all of the following, as appropriate: an evaluation of the whole school, improved functioning of the school, improved quality of pupil learning and in-service plans. The product should be free from accountability overtones, but it may be used in this way if it is appropriate and if the teachers are involved in the decisions about dissemination.

EVALUATE

Both the process and the product will need to be evaluated using one of the methods of evaluating evaluations from the previous chapter.

ACTION

The final stage is one of action following the evaluation. It is important that this action is built in as it is probably the most difficult stage. The same stages can be used as for the evaluation – choose a method for introducing the action, plan it, execute it, evaluate and monitor the process.

Action is concerned with the management of change of which, in essence, there are three stages:

- Where are we now?
- Where do we want to be?
- How do we get there?

An expansion of this process is given by Day, Johnston and Whitaker in their book *Managing Primary Schools: A Professional Development Approach*:

- reflect on practice
- share practice
- identify issues for change which may arise from the first two
- generate alternative strategies for change
- acquire the appropriate help to achieve this, both human and material
- apply the strategies
- evaluate the processes and outcomes.

In conclusion to this section of the Five Stage Guide, and before other methods are considered, some questions will need to be posed if real action is to result:

- What help and support do individuals or groups need
  a) from inside
  b) from outside the school?
  Can this be made available?
- What are the priorities for action?
- What is appropriate at this time, at this stage of development?
- Is the activity practical in terms of time, energy and resources?
- What will the teachers gain from the activity?

Interdependence between teachers rather than **de**pendence on others or **in**dependence, 'going solo', is thus a central feature in the action stage or the change process.

Having considered a general **PROCESS** method, the chapter will continue with a number of specific methods of whole school evaluation.

SCHOOL BASED REVIEW (SBR)

The International School Improvement Project (ISIP) is organised under the aegis of the Centre for Educational Research and Innovation (CERI) of the Organisation for Economic Co-operation and Development (OECD). It is a collaborative project involving institutions and individuals from fourteen countries which aims, through seminars, publications and other means, to develop and disseminate useful knowledge about the process of school improvement. The definition of **'school improvement'** adopted by ISIP in van Velzen et al. *Making School Improvement Work* is 'A systematic, sustained effort aimed at change in learning conditions and other related internal conditions in one or more schools, with the ultimate aim of accomplishing educational goals more effectively'.

SBR is thus seen as a school based diagnostic activity initiated for school development purposes. Their approach to SBR implies that it should be considered as a school improvement strategy in itself.

SBR can be said to have at least six characteristics:

1. It is a systematic process, not simply reflection.
2. Its short-term goal is to obtain valid information about a school's or department's condition, functions, purposes and products (effectiveness).
3. The review leads to action on an aspect of the school's organisation or curriculum.
4. It is a group activity that involves participants in a collegial process.
5. Optimally the process is 'owned' by the school or subsystem.
6. Its purpose is school improvement/development and it is a phase in that process.

THE MATRIX CONCEPT

Bollen & Hopkins in *School Based Review: Towards a Praxis* state that one of the lessons they have learnt from their work on SBR during ISIP is that it is difficult to ensure that action or development result from review. In the attempt to bridge the gap between review and development, they developed a matrix to assist in the execution of SBR efforts. One of the key elements in linking review to development is planning on the basis of a clear perception of the process and role. The matrix arrangement identifies the major roles involved in SBR, the main components of the SBR process and defines the relationship between them. The matrix is a conceptual framework for thinking about SBR, a planning and evaluation tool for doing SBR and it also provides a basis for dialogue with practitioners. The full matrix diagram is included at the end of this section.

The cells produced by the interaction of the axes contain potentially both **ROLES** (as defined by the horizontal axis) and **ACTIVITIES** (as defined by the vertical axis). These cells represent the totality of the SBR experience, but, of course, not every cell is represented in any one SBR project. Bollen & Hopkins suggest it is as a means of understanding, planning, evaluating, comparing and discussing different SBR efforts that the matrix has potential value. The matrix, though, is not intended as a prescriptive straightjacket. It is designed to assist those starting the SBR process in developing a policy and support structure for SBR and in identifying training needs.

The collective ISIP experience of SBR in a variety of member countries points to the following tentative conclusions:

- SBR requires that teachers be trained for it. Precisely how and in what way is not clear. A search for objectivity is the keynote.

- SBR requires that schools devote a substantial amount of time, energy and resources to it. Nowhere has it succeeded as a 'fringe' activity. In its idealised form, SBR requires (or perhaps creates) idealised schools in which collegiality, co-operation, open communications and fraternity rule and where professional development and professional self-respect go hand in hand. Even in its more instrumental form SBR requires that resources for improvement be made available. Nor is it remotely a successful means of enforcing 'standards' on teachers. Any close association between contractual accountability and SBR leads to the impoverishment of the latter and to an ineffective assertion of the former.

In summary, SBR presumes a highly professional teaching force—well trained in the skills of institution review, aware of its own professionality, possessed of the high morale necessary to seek for constant improvement and confident of support in what they desire from the other stakeholders in education.

The full matrix by Bollen & Hopkins, included at the end of the section, is rather complex. A simplified version may be of more use in primary schools.

If the horizontal axis is considered in the first instance, the questions of:

Who, or what, is	SUBJECT to review?
Who is	DOING the review?
Who is	MANAGING the review?
Who is	SUPPORTING the review?
Who is	CONTROLLING the review?
Who, or what, is	INFLUENCING the review?

may be answered by giving the WHO (actual names), or the WHAT (areas, activities, or processes). This may well be sufficient to assist in focussing a review. An example of this might be as follows:

Who or what are **Subject** to review	Who is **Doing** the review	Who is **Managing** the review	Who is **Supporting** the review	Who is **Controlling** the review	Whoor what is **Influencing** the review
The Maths scheme	All Staff	Ms. Smith	Ms. Jones Mr. Gov	Ms. Jones	Must be completed this term

This may, however, be expanded to the ROLE, that is the part to be played, and the FUNCTION, that is the work involved, rather than on particular individuals. An example of this might be as follows:

Who or what are **Subject** to review	Who is **Doing** the review	Who is **Managing** the review	Who is **Supporting** the review	Who is **Controlling** the review	Whoor what is **Influencing** the review
The Maths scheme	All Staff	Maths Co-ord	Head Governors	Head	Must be completed this term

In the simplified version, any headings which are seen to be helpful may be put in a **PROCESS** column.

It may be useful as a further stage to use the major headings of what needs to be considered:

The **START CONDITIONS** are the past experience or history of the school in relation to review and what needs to be done to bring the school to a state of readiness for the review.

The **PREPARATION** phase refers to those activities that ensure readiness for the review process and if the decision to proceed is made what training might be necessary.

The **REVIEW (INITIAL)** phase involves gathering general information about the school's organisation and curriculum.

The **REVIEW (SPECIFIC)** phase involves the setting of priorities for an in depth review of particular aspects of the school.

In the **DEVELOPMENT** phase decisions on policy are taken in the light of the findings from previous phases and an implementation plan is put into effect.

The SBR process can be said to be institutionalised when a school's organisational norms, climate or culture involves activities in other areas.

Not all of the sections have to be completed, only those which are appropriate. Another method is to put a tick or cross in the cells which need to be considered and then to enlarge on these cells on separate sheets of paper. An example of this might be as shown below:

Who or what are **Subject** to review	Who is **Doing** the review	Who is **Managing** the review	Who is **Supporting** the review	Who is **Controlling** the review	Who or what is **Influencing** the review
The maths scheme					Was completed two years ago
Read Present Scheme	All staff	Maths Co-ord	Head Governors	Head	Must be completed this week
What is happening now	All Classes	Maths Co-ord	Head	Head	By end of half term
Year 4	Yrs 2, 3, 4 teachers	Maths Co-ord			By end of half term
	As necessary				Next academic year

Once these major headings have been used it may be worthwhile to proceed to the subheadings of the full matrix (page 69).

The matrix, therefore, is a **planning tool** not a specific model or approach. It is prescriptive. It is designed to help those responsible for implementing SBR to understand the process by providing a detailed analysis and also acts as an aide-mémoire and basis for comparison. If it helps you, then use it in any way that suits you, but if you do not find it useful, and this applies to all the suggested methods of whole school evaluation being made here, then adapt it or devise a method of your own.

GUIDELINES FOR REVIEW AND INTERNAL DEVELOPMENT IN SCHOOLS (GRIDS)

There are now four handbooks, both primary and secondary in phases one and two. It is important that the *Primary School Handbook second edition* is used as this incorporates the accumulated experience of the project, over the period 1981 to 1988, about the conditions which are necessary for schools to develop successfully. This GRIDS handbook has been used for much of what follows. The climate in education has changed dramatically since the first editions of the GRIDS handbooks were published in 1984. The second edition takes account of the increased role of governors and parents, the pressure for greater accountability and the impact of the National Curriculum. Primary schools need to rethink, develop and change in response to these new circumstances. The advice contained in this handbook provides a solid framework for this task.

Key points about the process are:

- Joint staff decisions produce more willingness to change than one person taking decisions and having to persuade others.
- Staff know what is expected of them.
- The process results in a sense of ownership by the teachers.
- There is an enhanced clarity of shared purpose.
- Manageable goals are identified.
- Consideration of staff development and in-service needs are incorporated into the process.
- The procedures can work in conjunction with many existing LEA schemes and checklists for school based review.

The Full School Based Review Matrix

Process	Subject to review	Doing the review	Managing the review	Supporting the review	Controlling the review	Influencing the review
Start Condition—Past Experience,						
Preparation (Readiness) Phase Initiation						
Negotiation over						
• participation						
• control						
• training						
Decision to proceed						
Review (Initial) Phase: Planning for Review						
Decision on Instrumentation						
Reporting of Findings						
Decision to Proceed						
Review (Specific) Phase: Setting Priorities						
Planning for Review						
Mobilisation of Resources/Expertise						
Training for Review						
Gathering Information						
Validating Conclusions						
Feedback & Evaluation						
Decision to Proceed						
Development Phase: Establishing Policy						
Planning for Implementation						
Training (Inset) for Implementation						
Implementation of Policy with particular reference to:						
• school organisation						
• materials						
• teaching style						
• knowledge utilisation						
• acceptance of change						
Monitoring and Evaluation						
Institutionalisation Phase: Monitoring of Action						
Utlisation of SBR Process in other areas of curriculum and school organisation						
Development of problem solving capacity as an organisational form within the school						

From the primary Headteachers' standpoint the attraction of GRIDS will probably lie in the following features:

- Systematic identification of priorities naturally leads to a school and staff development plan
- INSET needs are identified
- GRIDS provides a well-tried tool for managing the curriculum and managing change.

The title of the project was carefully chosen. Firstly, the materials are *guidelines*: they contain structured step-by-step advice about how to conduct a school review and development exercise. Schools are not expected to follow these suggestions slavishly but rather adapt and amend as required. Secondly, the focus is on school *review* leading to internal school development and not something that stops short at the review stage. Thirdly, the word *internal* indicates that the review is not for external accountability purposes. Fourthly, the word *developmental* emphasises the developmental nature of the review. The word *school* emphasises that GRIDS is directed at the whole school rather than individual teachers or small groups.

These original aims have been modified and re-thought in the light of the experience gained to date.

GRIDS KEY PRINCIPLES

- The GRIDS process is first and foremost intended to be a whole school process.
- The main purpose is to move beyond a review stage into development for internal school improvement and not to produce a report for accountability purposes.
- The process should be jointly controlled by the school Head and staff, with a realistic appreciation of the necessary relationships with governors, parents and the LEA.

GRIDS' SECONDARY PRINCIPLES

- **Control:** Decisions about what happens to any information or reports generated in the GRIDS process should rest with the teachers and others involved. The Head and teachers should decide whether and how to involve the other groups in the school such as pupils, parents, advisers and governors.

- **Involvement:** The staff of the school should be consulted and involved in the review and development process as much as possible. Genuine consultation and involvement of staff are necessary if teachers are to commit themselves to implementing changes in their schools.
- **External help:** It is strongly recommended that experienced outsiders should be invited to provide help and advice both on the process of GRIDS itself and as 'experts' to help specific developments when the school has decided the priorities.
- **Resources:** The demands made on key resources like time, money and skilled personnel should be realistic and feasible for schools and LEAs.
- **Accountability:** Engagement in the GRIDS process cannot relieve staff of the need to be accountable to pupils and parents, to fellow teachers and to their employers. However, it requires an initial staff review of all school activities, and aims for developmental changes so that the school accomplishes its goals more effectively. Therefore, doing GRIDS should help schools answer calls to be accountable in their own terms.

Probably the most significant of these, it has been suggested, is the principle that all teachers should be consulted and involved in the exercise as much as possible. The second edition also offers a significant change concerning the role of governors, parents and consultants. Other major changes are concerned with the role of the Head, the time span for a complete cycle and the establishment for criteria for judging effectiveness.

The central practical recommendation in the GRIDS method is that schools should not attempt to review everything at once. Instead, the recommended procedure is i) to take a look at what is happening in the school, ii) on the basis of this to identify one or two areas that the staff consider to be priorities for specific review and development, iii) tackle these first, iv) evaluate what has been achieved and then v) select another priority area. The five stages of the cyclical process are shown on page 72.

McMahon writing in the *World Yearbook of Education 1986* explains that the process appeared to work best in those schools where:

- the basic principles underlying the exercise were clearly agreed
- a timetable was drawn up and adhered to

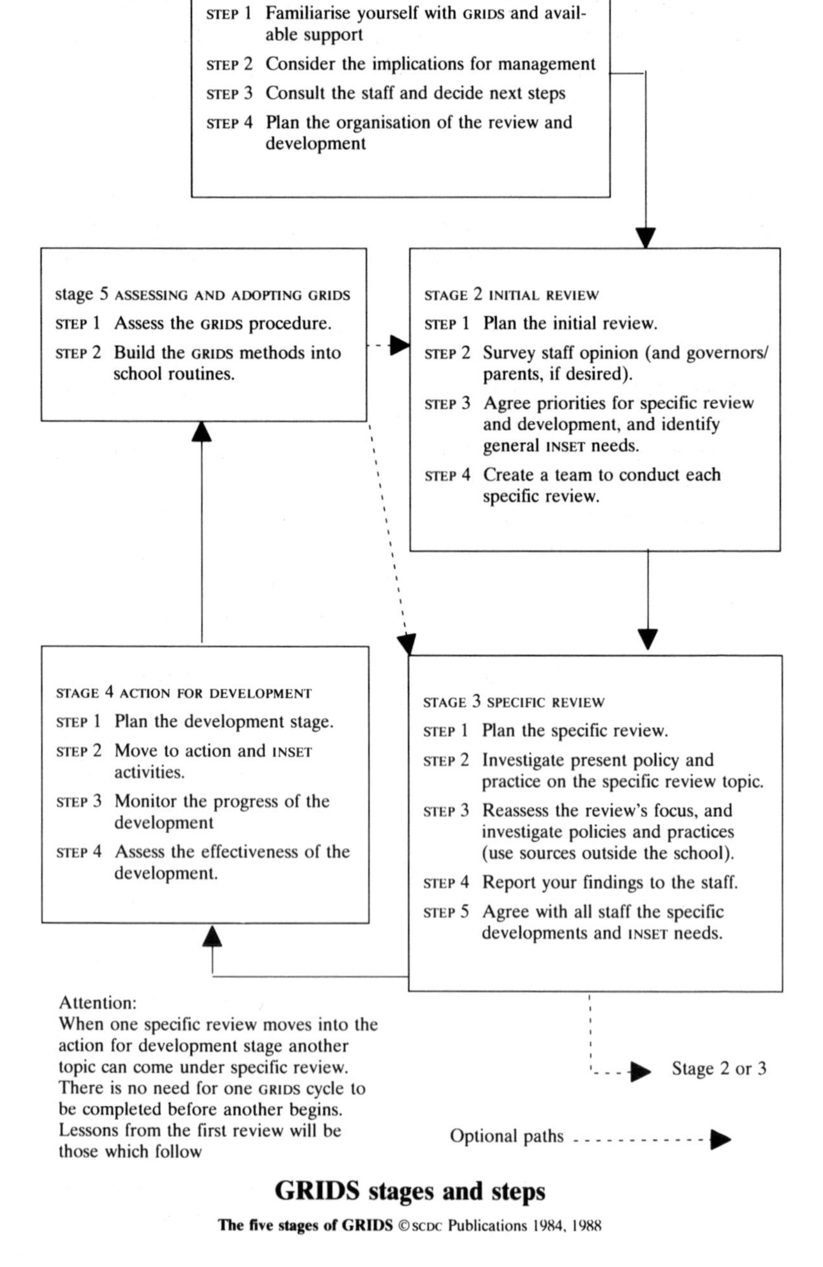

GRIDS stages and steps

The five stages of GRIDS

- the co-ordinator ensured the whole process was carefully planned and monitored and the momentum sustained
- the leaders of the working groups had status in the organisation and the groups were integrated into the existing decision-making machinery of the school
- appropriate methods of collecting and analysing data were selected.

Phase II of GRIDS has provided lessons both for curriculum developers in general and for those interested in SBR in particular, write McMahon, Holly and Steadman in the ISIP publication *School Based Review: Towards a Praxis.* Attention here is confined to the lessons most relevant for the development of SBR.

- SBR requires an atmosphere of co-operative endeavour, not only within the schools which are expected to take on the process, but also in the educational system which supports the schools.
- School autonomy cannot be total, and perhaps in hindsight the emphasis given to school control during the initial phase of GRIDS did not sufficiently separate control of the internal GRIDS process from questions of control of the priorities chosen for review. In order to engender commitment for change, it is still the GRIDS team's view that the school staff must make the final decisions on the priority of review and development. However, it is clear that the initial review stage now ought to deliberately incorporate consideration of what parents, school governors and different levels of government would present as priority issues.
- The GRIDS team is still concerned at an apparent lack of rigour and objectivity in many review and development procedures. The word 'apparent' is emphasised because experience indicates that the action orientation of school does not result purely from an oversimplification of the process or a resistance to examining present practices critically. Both these factors may be present, but others add to the problems. To ask schools to produce clear criteria by which to judge their effectiveness is to set a complex task under the guise of apparent simplicity.
- Schools which have worked through more than one cycle of GRIDS demonstrate a sequence growth. The first cycle serves to generate shared experiences, teamwork, ownership of the

process and confidence. Realistically it is in the second and subsequent cycles that one should expect increased rigour in procedures, application of clear criteria to present practices, greater openness to involving consultants and others, and a readiness to cope with the external pressures for accountability.

- Finally, it is clear that the GRIDS' process itself, as now described in the published handbooks, is capable of streamlining and improvement to show more clearly how SBR has potential for coping with demands for change identified both from within and from outside schools.

Amongst many of the interesting observations which are made by Constable, Brown & Williams in *An Evaluation of the Implementation of GRIDS in one Local Education Authority* the common recommendations were:

- Read and frequently reconsult the materials, since they contain a great deal of carefully thought-out advice.
- Get clear about the advantages of GRIDS.
- Follow the procedure outlined.
- Take seriously the task of working in groups with other teachers.
- Understand the value of outside help and use it.
- Expect to learn from the initial use of GRIDS.

INTERNATIONAL MOVEMENTS TOWARDS EDUCATIONAL CHANGE (IMTEC)/ SCHOOL DEVELOPMENT GUIDE (SDG)

IMTEC—International Movements Towards Educational Change—is a non-profit foundation committed to helping institutions improve their work and practice. IMTEC was established originally in the early 1970s as a project of the Organisation for Economic Co-operation and Development (OECD) for the express purpose of coming to grips with the management of educational change. In 1977, IMTEC became independent of OECD, but has retained much of its original mission of studying change and helping institutions and individuals in countries throughout the world define, initiate and carry through educational innovations. The National Foundation for Educational Research (NFER) in England and Wales decided in 1982 to adapt and test an existing IMTEC

Institutional Development Plan (IDP) which has become the School Development Guide (SDG). Accompanying the SDG is a computer program on disk written for the BBC model B micro. The program allows for data to be input and analyses produced without undue delay by the staff of the school involved.

The IMTEC/IDP is an intervention strategy which is designed to help educational institutions undertake a comprehensive self-assessment and self-development process. A major aim is to help diagnose their situation as a prelude to specific evaluations which will lead to adjustments in working methods, school organisation and climate. The School Development Guide (SDG) is an instrument that allows teachers' perceptions and views to be surveyed, so that the resultant feedback may identify starting points in the school development process.

The SDG measures a wide spectrum of factors relevant to primary schools which does not serve as a prescription of action or change to be undertaken, but as a springboard to analysis of the school situation, including underlying features, out of which will come proposals by the school staff for particular developments.

The process may be summarised in nine principal stages, as follows:

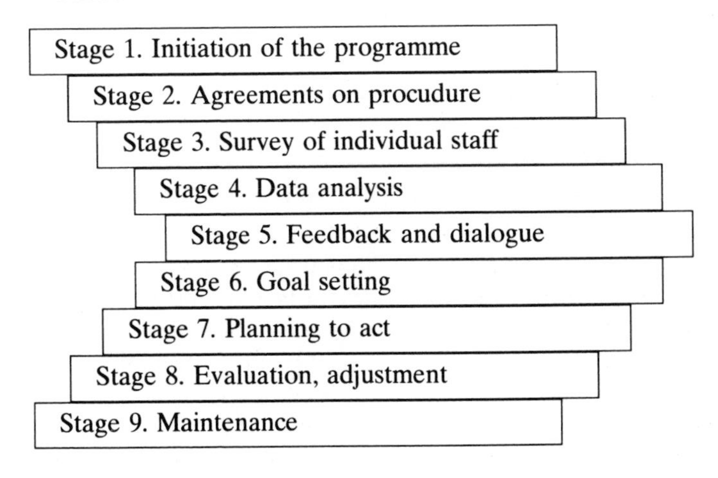

The main instrument is a long questionnaire which takes about forty minutes to complete. The content of this questionnaire has been checked to ensure that it covers features which research has indicated are important. These include:

- classroom management and school discipline
- school management and leadership
- goal definition and monitoring
- staff development and LEA support
- parental and community involvement.

Twelve scales are embodied in the instrument. Each scale is designed to provide some information concerning one of the factors in the school. The headings are:

- Values and Goals
- Objectives of the School as a Whole
- Staff Relationships and Co-operation
- School Climate
- Leadership and Management
- Decision-making
- Communication
- Influences on the School
- Assessment and Evaluation
- Changes in the School
- Teaching Methods
- Teacher Activities.

The responses to the questions are recorded on the questionnaire first for a teacher's perception of the *actual* state, then for their view of the *ideal* state, that is, what ought to be the state of things.

Full details are given on how to administer, analyse and present the data in a simple and easy-to-follow book. This is followed by feedback sessions which are designed to prompt questioning and discussion aimed at identifying matters of concern. The final stages of Goal Setting, Planning for Action and Long-term School Development are then completed followed by Evaluation and Maintenance.

DIAGNOSING INDIVIDUAL AND ORGANISATIONAL NEEDS—DION

DION—Diagnosing Individual and Organisational Needs—is an approach for identifying in-service training needs at the organisational level rather than at the individual level. The basic tool of analysis is the Diagnostic Inventory for Individual and Organisational Needs which covers the following issues:

- Aims and values
- Resources
- Staff recruitment and selection
- Organisational structure and roles
- Leadership
- Motivation
- Teamwork and conflict
- Creativity
- Problem solving and coping
- Staff development and INSET
- Relationship with the environment.

Staff are asked to respond to the sixty-six statements in the inventory individually although this may be done in a group setting. The results are transferred onto an individual grid which may then be summarised on a group summary sheet. This summary highlights the particular areas which the staff perceive as problems and assists in the prioritisation of areas of the school which might require attention. The next stages are of solution building, action planning, implementation and evaluation.

The DION inventory is quick to administer and collate and does involve all the staff in the process. DION was deliberately devised to be a negative instrument with the statements themselves being couched in the negative, concerning what is *not* being done in the school and the whole inventory concentrates on the problems in the school.

Many groups of teachers from a variety of schools with whom this inventory has been administered by myself, however, feel that it might be a better instrument if it emphasised the positive rather than the negative, factors.

THE ROLE OF CRITICAL COLLEAGUES

In this section there will be an introduction followed by:

- Arranging the circle
- Organising the evaluation process
- Evaluating the evaluation process
- Continuation.

INTRODUCTION

As well as a group of Critical Colleagues this activity is also called Critical Friends or Critical Circles, even a Circle of Critical Colleagues. Whatever it is called, all are basically similar. This activity can be carried out at the same time, before or after, any of the other methods given in this chapter. Indeed, it might be seen as desirable or even necessary, for schools and those in them to be exposed to a variety of approaches to school evaluation.

Critical Colleagues has been used most successfully with Headteachers, but it has also worked well with deputies, curriculum co-ordinators and classroom teachers. It is particularly useful and helpful to those in small schools, especially rural schools where teachers more commonly work in isolation. It is here that the sharing and resolution of problems relating to the National Curriculum, school management or reception may be most needed.

ARRANGING THE CIRCLE

This may be arranged as the result of:

- a perceived need
- attendance on a course
- a different type of grouping
- by invitation
- self-selecting.

Whichever way the group comes together the following points will need to be borne in mind when setting up a circle or group:

- **Trust** is an essential element. This takes time to develop, but selection of those with whom you feel this a likely outcome must be considered at the outset. Certainly the converse is true, do not become involved with those where you feel that trust will not develop.

- **Close personal friends** at the beginning of the process are unlikely to provide the best people for a circle. For although there might, initially, be the element of trust, it may be too 'cosy' or you may not want to hurt a friend's feelings by being 'honest'. It is also potentially threatening to the rest of the group to have those who know each other very well, consequently some members feel excluded.
- **Neighbouring catchment areas** need to be considered for similar reasons, but in this case it may be that you are in 'competition' with each other, so would not want to be too close.
- **Mixture of schools**, classes or subject areas need to be looked at. Do you want everybody from the same type or size of schools or not? Similarly with age groups taken or subject areas.
- **Size of the group** is not normally something which causes difficulty. Anything between three and six seems to work with four, perhaps, being the best.
- **Funding** may or may not be a major item, but travelling can be expensive. It is often possible to use in-service days or 'after school' time, because if supply teachers are needed then funding does become a problem.
- **Time** is related to the previous item and is selected for any of the activities involved, but this is also related to **frequency** of meetings. Initially, one round of meetings is enough to set up, then go from there.
- **Use of consultants, outsiders** may be helpful in providing an 'external audit' and avoiding 'cosiness', but it may contrast with the element of trust which was the first item on this list.
- **The main objective** of the group and intervisiting is that **you**, personally, should feel some benefit from the **process** itself of visiting other schools. Others may also benefit from visiting your school to see how you do things.

ORGANISING THE EVALUATION PROCESS

BEFORE the visits take place you will need a number of meetings to work out:

- **WHAT** you are going to evaluate
- Negotiate what you are going to look at and establish criteria
- **HOW** you are going to do it

In other words, what are the objectives of the activity?

There are decisions which need to be made as a group such as:

- How much time you will spend in the schools.
- How much time discussing it afterwards?
- Where will this discussion take place?
- Whether or not the head of the school should be present whilst you visit and what his/her role should be.
- Should the children be present or is this just for teachers?
- The political aspects of intervisiting need to be taken into account and the feeling and views of those teachers *not* involved.
- Schools need to be prepared for each visitation.
- Is the order of visiting significant?
- What needs to be done before the visit, e.g. preparation of copies of any school documentation which might be considered to be appropriate?
- Who will be seen? Children, members of staff, teachers?

DURING the visits, these points may be of some use:

- Try not to look at too many different aspects of the school. It is probably better to look at *one* aspect in some depth, rather than a number of things superficially.
- Keep it as simple as possible.
- It is not necessary to look at the *same* thing in each school.
- What do you record at the time, if anything?

AFTER the visits
You will want to share some of your experiences with the rest of the group.

- **HOW** do you share your observations with each other?
- **WHAT** do you share of your observations with each other?
- You will probably want to be as 'honest' as you can. Try to be as helpful and positive as you can; refer to strengths rather than any perceived weaknesses.
- Do you keep a written record?
- What **ACTION** is planned as a group or as an individual?

You will find you improve as the visits proceed, in that you are able to observe and absorb more each visit. Initial fears about the whole process are usually unfounded. You will develop trust and friendship of a group of fellow colleagues which will probably go some way to relieving the stress of the post you are in and any isolation you may have had. You may be surprised how exhausting the nature of this activity is, but, hopefully, it will be worthwhile for all concerned.

EVALUATING THE EVALUATION PROCESS
This process of evaluating the evaluation has been considered in some depth elsewhere, but it is still essential that this is carried out in some detail. In addition it is likely that there will be:

- an increased awareness of one's own and others' practice
- an increased awareness of the need to evaluate further and in greater depth
- a willingness to try to implement new ideas or ideas for improvement which have been considered but 'delayed' in their implementation
- a 'resolution' to take action.

CONTINUATION

Dependent on the above evaluation of the process is the question about whether or not there will be a further 'cycle' or plans for the future, perhaps in the form of regular meetings or different activities. Some groups 'die' after the first round, others last for a number of years. The main factors seem to be about whether the 'need' is still there and how the personalities mix.

DO-IT-YOURSELF—DIY

This is an approach which has been developed by Barry Mountford at Crewe+Alsager Faculty of Manchester Metropolitan University to assist in school diagnosis as a prelude to:

- identifying school INSET needs
- the formulation of a School Development Plan (SDP).

STAGES IN THE PROCESS

- Identify key areas contributing to school effectiveness. Examples might be subject areas or cross curricular issues.
- Write the name of each 'key area' agreed or identified on to a postcard.
- Each member of staff in turn takes the cards and sorts them as follows:

  Clear 'strengths' are front grouped.

  Clear 'weaknesses' are back grouped.

  The 'grey areas', where there is no definite strength or weakness form a third set.

  Within each set (strength, weakness and grey area) re-sort the order:

  The strongest strength becomes the first card in the pack and the weakest weakness becomes the last in the pack.

  Each member of staff ends up with a set of ordered cards which is a ranking statement of the individual's view of the state of the school.
- Individual diagnostic statements are then collated on a matrix. The size of the matrix will depend on the number of 'key areas'.

This yields a pictorial representation of the staff's perception on the state of the school. Clustering or dispersal on any of the 'key areas' is used for a basis for discussion and action.

FURTHER POINTS

Should the process of identifying the 'key areas' be a co-operative activity involving all the staff? If so it will need to be managed.

When the agreed key areas have been transferred onto cards, is it desirable or necessary to explain each key area?

To aid in the analysis of the school it might be necessary to have more than one set of cards. For example it might be desirable to separate 'organisation and management' from 'curriculum' areas.

	STAFF RANKING OF 'KEY AREAS'									
KEY AREA	1	2	3	4	5	6	7	8	9	10
A										
B										
C										
D										
E										
F										
G										
H										
I										
J										

If this is done might it be a good idea to have these different sets of cards colour coded?

The *physical* process of sorting the cards seems to help the *thinking* processes involved in the individual's view of the priorities within the school.

This exercise of ranking and comparing of views enables discussion and the beginnings of the formulation of an agreed development plan for the staff of the school and an identification of its related INSET needs.

Th strengths of this essentially simple process are that it involves all the staff not only in deciding the areas which are to be considered, but also in physically sorting these areas into a ranked order. These processes help in the 'ownership' of any outcome as each stage has been decided by the staff themselves.

ADDITIONAL METHODS

This section reinforces the idea that those methods of whole school evaluation which have been described are not an exclusive list by any means. Additional methods which may be encountered include:

- LEA evaluation schemes
- the ILEA checklist
- taking professional stock
- SWOT
- The use of OFSTED materials.

LEA EVALUATION SCHEMES

Many LEAs have developed their own whole school evaluation schemes for use in their own authorities. Some of the pioneers in this field were Oxfordshire and Solihull, Warwickshire. These have since become too numerous to mention. Where an authority scheme exists, however, it may be considered to be either inappropriate or undesirable to introduce any alternative methods of whole school evaluation.

THE ILEA CHECKLIST

The checklist produced by the ILEA (Inner London Education Authority) in 1977 was one of the first schemes to suggest any systematic process of self-evaluation, by looking at:

- What you are doing
- Why you are doing it
- Whether you are doing it well
- Whether you ought to be doing something different

It was presented as a basis for the development of a school's own form of self-assessment, to be modified or extended to suit the intentions and interests of the individual school. It was also suggested that the answers to the questions would promote discussion both within the school and with the inspectorate so that schools 'may have the benefit of an external viewpoint to put beside their own'.

The checklist itself consists of a series of questions under the headings:

- The Children
- Parental and Community Involvement
- Managers (now of course Governors)
- Programmes (Schemes) of Work or Guidelines
- Class Organisation
- Attainment
- Staffing
- Staff Meetings
- Simple Statistics
- General Environment
- Action
- Questions for the Headteacher to ask himself or herself
- Questions for the individual teacher to ask himself or herself
- The acid test!

A more recent up-to-date checklist is the one produced by Wiltshire County Council entitled *Self Evaluation in the Primary School.*

TAKING PROFESSIONAL STOCK

Paisey and Paisey in *Effective Management in Primary Schools* give a process for a detailed systematic method for primary Headteachers to take stock of their own managerial performance. The ratings of one hundred items allows Work Output to be balanced against Interpersonal Relations. It also considers the ten managerial performance categories of:

- Physical assets
- School climate
- Values and objectives
- Curriculum content and development
- Organisation, care and development of children
- Staff structure and deployment
- Financial systems management
- Standards of performance
- External relations
- Managerial skills

This may assist Headteachers to reflect on their own management expertise in a professional review, allow for a project management review and consider their own career development.

SWOT

SWOT stands for a technique which is most useful in examining the *Strengths, Weaknesses, Opportunities* and *Threats* to the school or an aspect of it. In essence it involves asking a series of questions and, more importantly, working together to provide some answers to those questions which might be:

STRENGTHS
What are the strongest points about your school?

WEAKNESSES
What are your weaknesses? Be as honest as you can!
What can be done to remedy them?

OPPORTUNITIES
What opportunities are there for you to 'improve' the school?
Are they being taken?
What about the **TIMING** of these new opportunities?

THREATS
What are the potential threats to your school?
Don't procrastinate—act!

It is better to concentrate on the positive aspects of the school. Try to emphasise the strengths and the opportunities rather than the negative side, the weaknesses and threats to the school. This is often an attitude of mind or a way of looking at things. For example if the numbers in the school are decreasing and class sizes falling, do not see this as negative, but rather, 'A strength of this school is that we have small classes and so we are able to give more individual attention to the children'.

THE USE OF OFFICE FOR STANDARDS IN EDUCATION (OFSTED) MATERIALS

In general terms this book is designed to give a number of **ALTERNATIVE** ideas and methods to the OFSTED inspections of schools. Nevertheless it is prudent for all those involved in schools to look at these materials in some depth. It is important to read *The Handbook for the Inspection of Schools* rather than merely *The Framework for the Inspection of Schools.* Two main reasons for reading the complete document are that *The Framework* does not include the 'Guidance' section (part 4 of *The Handbook*), nor does it include the 'Technical Papers' (part 5). BOTH these sections need to be read in conjunction with *The Framework* if full benefit is to be gained from it.

The Framework gives the very important 'Evaluation Criteria'. These criteria are detailed and very well thought out as would be expected. The Guidance section gives the even more important 'Amplification of evaluation criteria' which are more detailed still and give the qualities of good and poor schools. The Technical Paper includes another important section for those who are involved in the evaluation of their own particular school – that of 'Evaluation Criteria – the Key Questions'. These questions are under the headings:

- What is the quality of assessment practice?
- What is the quality of record keeping?
- What is the quality of reporting to parents?
- What is the quality of the school's management of assessment, recording and reporting?

The whole of the documentation needs to be read in detail, but it may be useful to give the structure of *The Framework* with a few comments.

Section 1 has a variety of mainly factual information about the school under the following headings:

1.1 Basic information about the school
1.2 Intake of pupils and the area served by the school
1.3 School data and indicators
1.4 Record of the evidence base of the inspection.

Section 2 is concerned with standards, quality, efficiency and ethos. The evaluation criteria consider the overall judgement about the school which should be based on evaluation of the quality of education provided, the standards of work, the efficiency of management and the effectiveness of the school community in providing for the spiritual, moral, social and cultural development of pupils.

Section 3 is about standards of achievement and quality of learning.

Section 4 covers the efficiency of the school which should be judged by

> 'the extent to which resources including time, money and staff, are used to maximise the achievement of the school's aims and objectives; the extent to which the school aligns its planning is to be judged by the extent to which the school has a means of evaluating its provision, identifying strengths and weaknesses, and maintaining a development plan to address priorities. Plans are assessed in terms of whether the priorities for action are appropriate; whether the implications for the development programme have been assessed (including an assessment of the costs, steps to be taken, staff to be involved and training needed); and whether criteria have been developed to evaluate success.'

The 'guidance' section of *The Handbook* gives amplification of the criteria the inspectors are looking for: where a school is well managed pupils learn effectively and efficiently.

> 'The leadership of the governing body and the headteacher gives a clear direction to the school's work. The school's aims are well publicised and translated into clear objectives with attainable targets. Priorities for development are based on sound evaluation and are reflected in the organisation of the school. The development and training of staff are clearly linked to their responsibilities. Pupils and staff understand what is expected of them, are well motivated and have high aspirations. The structures and systems which enable pupils and staff to work effectively are in place and are regularly monitored. Lines of communication are clear. The school community is orderly, has positive attitudes to work and sound relationships. Parents are well informed and confident about the school and their child's progress. Finance is efficiently managed and focused on clear priorities for the provision of resources.
>
> Where management is unsatisfactory pupils' learning is ineffective or is achieved inefficiently. The school lacks purpose and provides little incentive to achieve. Aims and policies have little effect on practice. Inefficient co-ordination of decisions

and actions limits effectiveness and leads to inadequate performance and poor deployment of resources, including staff. Attitudes and behaviour are adversely affected and although poor management and low standards are not necessarily connected it is likely that standards will not adequately reflect the pupil's abilities.

There are few aspects of the work of the school which do not reflect the quality of the management.'

This sentiment, also a theme of this book, cannot be emphasised too much. The 'match' between the school's actual practice and the intentions expressed in the documentation is a theme which runs through the whole of the OFSTED materials.

The materials also home in on an element with which I would agree wholeheartedly, namely 'hardest to locate but vital to trace are the effects of management and planning on the quality of teaching and learning, and on the quality of the daily life and experience of pupils and staff.' In order to assist in the location of these effects the materials include 'some useful enquiries' which include the following questions to be asked:

- Do the governors and senior management have a clear sense of purpose and direction for the school?
- Does the leadership make the best of the people and resources available?
- Does the quality of management and planning promote positive attitudes to teaching and learning?
- Are the school's values, plans and procedures expressed in clear policies and documentation?
- How closely does the day-to-day reality of life in the school correspond to the school's declared intentions?
- How consistent are standards, provision, and the degree of satisfaction experienced by all pupils and staff?

Section 6 also includes a section on the school's organisation and administration which 'should be judged in terms of the efficiency and effectiveness of its routine administrative procedures and operations, its systems for communication of information to pupils, staff and parents and the use made of information technology, in clearly identified distribution of responsibilities and duties and in a well-planned daily routine.'

It is interesting to note that two factors to be taken into account in the school's organisation and administration are the use of information technology in terms of its contribution to the efficiency and effectiveness of the school and the effectiveness of communication in small primary schools where it will often be informal and face-to-face.

Resources and their management is the final part of section A of *The Handbook*, and includes teaching and support staff. Staffing is to be evaluated in relation to three features:

1. **Management:** the extent to which there are adequate arrangements for recruitment, retention, motivation and reward of staff members.
2. **Deployment:** the extent to which the deployment of teachers and allocation of responsibilities contribute to achieving the overall aims and objectives of the school; the effectiveness of support staff and the extent to which they enhance the work of teachers and contribute to the purposes of the school.
3. **Development:** the extent to which there are effective arrangements to extend the knowledge and skills of teachers, and other staff where appropriate, and appraisal arrangements to provide a realistic picture of the effectiveness of their work and to support their professional development.

Other areas considered are resources for learning, accommodation, pupils' support and guidance, community links and liaison with other schools.

Part B of *The Framework* is concerned with subjects of the curriculum.

SOME FURTHER ISSUES

In this section it is planned to look at some of the issues and the related questions about whole school evaluation which have not been considered earlier.

CLIMATE

Many of the methods considered earlier in this chapter include in their introductions something to the effect that 'the climate has to be right before starting whole school evaluation'. The question which needs asking, therefore, is, 'Is it *ever* the "right" time?' The answer to this could well be, 'No', so you might as well go ahead anyway. It is probably better to ask 'How do you create the right climate in school for evaluation?' It seems to me that this requires a good deal of sensitivity to people's feelings by the manager. This leads to the second point.

RELATIONSHIPS

PEOPLE are involved in the process of evaluation. Personal relationships are very important. Evaluation may disrupt the relationship between members of staff and also between the Head and the staff. The manager should be aware of this possibility and plan for it.

SMALL SCHOOLS

What are the particular problems of small schools? How can these be overcome? Most of the methods described previously in the chapter are designed for schools of all sizes, but GRIDS has a chapter on small schools and there are differences which need to be recognised.

IMPROVEMENT ON THE SECOND CYCLE

Not surprisingly evaluation is something at which we get better with practice and experience. In the first cycle of an evaluation we are more likely to be concerned with outcomes, whereas in the second cycle there is more concern with process than product. If schools initiate evaluations in response to their *own* needs, which may or may not include producing accounts for outside audiences, these efforts are likely to be more sustained, to reflect actual experience of schools and to lead to a quality control which is in the hands of the teachers and Heads who have the prime responsibility for educating children and running schools.

3
Classroom Based Evaluation

For most teachers who spend most, if not all, of their time in the classroom, this chapter on classroom based evaluation is probably the most practical of all. As many different techniques as possible have been offered in order to assist the teacher to evaluate his or her own practice where it matters—in the classroom. The information will be of use to others such as Headteachers, governors and parents as it applies to their *managing* the evaluation of this area of the school. The chapter will include:

- some reasons for classroom based evaluation
- five different frameworks for asking evaluation questions
- a list of techniques with brief comments
- a longer look at partnerships and paired observations
- some of the problems involved with any or all classroom based evaluation
- management issues.

SOME REASONS FOR CLASSROOM BASED EVALUATION

Classroom self-evaluation by the teacher can be seen as a form of action-research in which the cycle of planning, action, reflection and analysis leads to re-planning, further action, reflection and analysis. This may be repeated as required. Another term which is often used is that of the 'reflective practitioner' which implies that the teachers do not merely engage in activity in the classroom, but also reflect on their practice.

The justification for ensuring teachers evaluate their own classroom practice systematically from time to time in order to increase professional effectiveness is based on three assumptions from Day, *Classroom-Based In-Service Teacher Education:*

- teachers cannot be developed by others, but only given opportunities to develop for themselves
- effective learning arises in response to the identification and confrontation of 'real' questions by the learner
- decisions about teaching should stem from reflection on the effects of previous actions.

All three of these may be helpful in energising the improvement of the teaching and learning process in an individual's classroom.

This type of evaluation is **NOT about teacher appraisal**, although this may become a significant part of a staff development programme.

It certainly is **teacher-centred**, that is self-centred, for the individual teacher lies at the heart of the process. This would seem to fit in with the culture of teacher classroom autonomy which has been, in the past, a strength of the British primary school system.

Classroom evaluation is **individual**. It is not necessarily across the whole staff and thus remains at the level of 'teacher activity' as opposed to a 'school activity'.

It is important that the teacher retains **ownership** of the activity and is able to control all aspects of what is being attempted.

While some of this activity takes place within pairs or groups, **individuals can use this assistance as they see fit** and can decide whether the activity is a group one or not. The aim of an 'outsider' is to act as a critical friend in order to facilitate the enlightenment and empowerment of the teacher. An external evaluation aims to be communicative, informative, interactive, insightful, consciousness raising, even critical, but above all, it aims to enhance and support the autonomous development of the learning, developing teacher.

The major justification for undertaking school self-evaluation is **enhanced professionalism** in the image and practice of teachers and schools. This self-evaluation is best introduced as a continuing part of professional practice, not as a short-term response to the introduction of teacher appraisal.

FIVE DIFFERENT FRAMEWORKS FOR ASKING EVALUATION QUESTIONS

The five different frameworks for asking questions are those of:

- Cronbach
- HMI
- Stake
- Open University
- Day, Johnston & Whitaker.

This assortment of frameworks is given so that the reader may have a variety of types of questions which may be asked and also a variety of styles from which to choose.

CRONBACH

The types of decision for which evaluation data may be collected as suggested by Cronbach are:

- **Course improvement**—deciding what teaching materials and methods are satisfactory and where change is needed.

- **Decisions about individuals**—identifying the needs of the pupil or the teacher for the purpose of planning his or her instruction, judging pupil or teacher merit for the purpose of selection and grouping, acquainting the pupil or teacher with his or her own progress and deficiencies.

- **Administrative regulation**—judging how good the system is, how good individual teachers are.

Decisions concerning which of these is to be selected for evaluation allow the teacher or manager to focus their attention.

HMI

HMI in their pamphlet *The curriculum from 5 to 16* say that assessment is inseparable from the teaching process since its prime purpose is to improve pupils' performance. It should help teachers to:

- diagnose pupils' strengths and weaknesses

- match the work of the classroom to their capabilities
- guide them into appropriate courses and groups
- involve them in discussion and self-appraisal
- inform their parents of progress reports and meetings.

A second purpose is to enable the teachers to see how far their objectives are being met and to adjust them and their teaching approaches accordingly. This is best done by reviewing pupils' progress in the light of what the teachers set out to do.

HMI continue that if schools are to fulfil these aims of assessment, development is needed in three main areas:

- clear definition of expectations as expressed through the aims and objectives of curricula and schemes of work
- improved methods of assessment in the classroom on a day-to-day basis
- improved methods of recording progress.

Much of the assessment described above has to go on in the busy environment of the classroom and must be largely impressionistic, though teachers need additional time to record these impressions.

From time to time also, informal assessment needs to be supported by more objective forms of testing, such as class tests and examinations devised by the teacher, which should be closely related to the work in hand.

Similarly, graded assessment, which has become common in recent years, should reflect the full range of classroom activities. Care must be taken to see that the tests do not dominate the work and that they do not so itemise the work that coherence is lost. Occasional use needs to be made of standardised tests, particularly tests of reading and numeracy, to help establish a base line of performance, for screening purposes, or for the diagnosis of particular difficulties. While these tests have the advantage of greater objectivity, they can too easily be divorced from classroom work and their use should be limited. This is particularly true for National Curriculum testing, for, whilst this is obligatory, it might easily become the be all and end all of classroom work.

STAKE

Stake in *Evaluating Educational Programmes* divided planning and teaching into three segments:

1. **Antecedents** – conditions which exist prior to teaching taking place, e.g. pupils' abilities, school and classroom context, resources, teaching organisation, etc.
2. **Transactions** – what happens between pupils and between teachers and pupils during the lesson.
3. **Outcomes** – what pupils learn (including unintended learning).

The idea is to compare the **INTENDED** antecedents, transactions or outcomes with the **OBSERVED** antecedents, transactions or outcomes. The congruence, or lack of it, between what was intended to happen and planned beforehand and what is observed in the classroom when this is put into practice should give plenty of food for thought.

Similar comparisons can be made between the **logical** contingency, or concurrence of events, in the intended planning and teaching in the left hand column and the **empirical** contingency in the observed antecedents, transactions or outcomes in the right hand column.

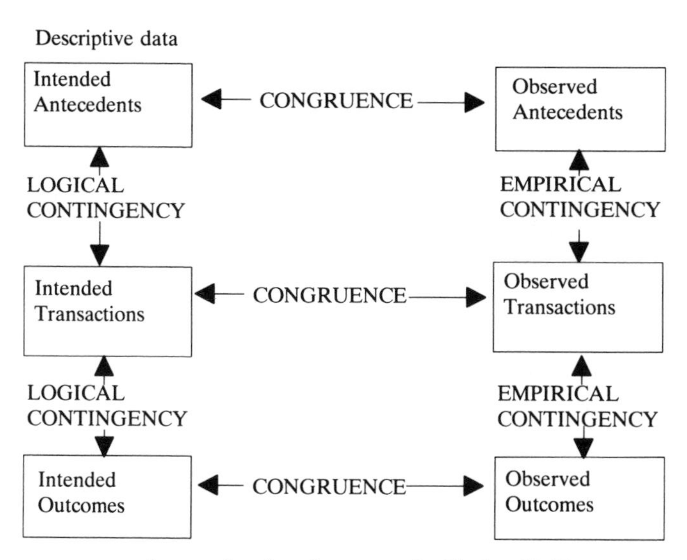

An evaluation framework (Stake 1967)

OPEN UNIVERSITY
Six questions which focus attention on the three central elements of classroom life—the pupils, the teacher and the task—are asked in the Open University course P234, which although written in 1980 are still worthwhile. They are:

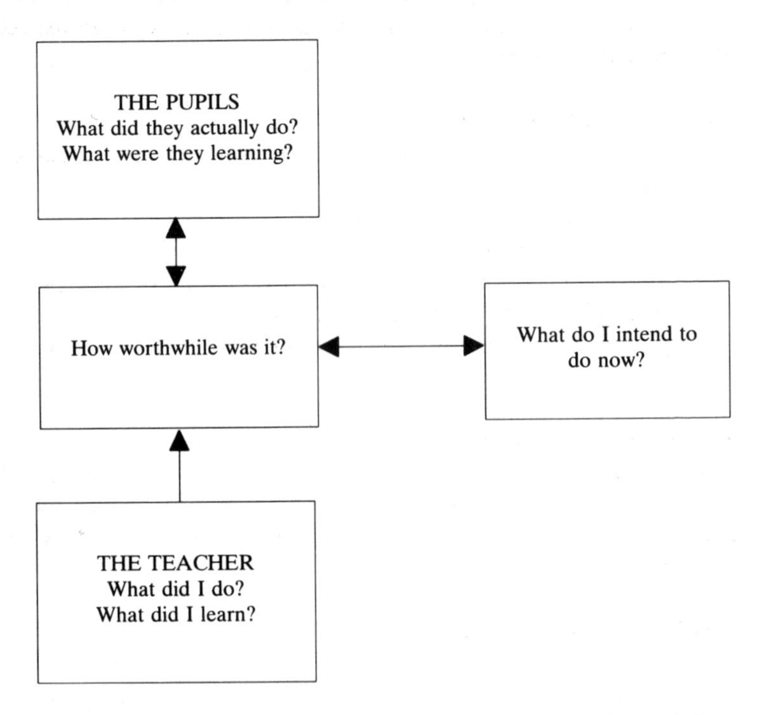

They are designed to ensure that the teacher moves through four distinct and necessary phases:

1. **Description** – identifying and selecting events.
2. **Interpretation** – assessing the consequences of these events.
3. **Judgement** – assessing how far these events were worthwhile.
4. **Decision** – accepting responsibility for 1-3 above and planning future action.

DAY, JOHNSTON & WHITAKER

Day, Johnston & Whitaker in *Managing Primary Schools: A Professional Development Approach* pose some questions concerning techniques for collecting classroom observations:

The WHY of observation

Decide what is the purpose. Is it primarily to solve a problem or to check on the effectiveness of a particular strategy or an aspect of curriculum content?

The WHAT of observation

This will be determined by the teacher's own interests, needs or concerns.

The WHO of observation

Teachers should beware of being over ambitious. For example, it may be sensible, if pupils are the focus, to observe one pupil or a small group; or if observing oneself it may be wise to focus on one aspect of teacher talk (e.g. questioning).

The WHEN of observation

Observation must be built in as a part of the teaching plan, and short concentrated periods of time for this, standing outside actual contact with pupils, may be more practical than long periods when the teacher is likely to be distracted.

The HOW of observation

Examples of techniques of collecting observations are given later. It is equally important, however, to find ways of organising the activity itself so that time and energy can be focused in support of the commitment; and frameworks for recording the information gained from classroom observations must also be devised.

A SUMMARY OF TECHNIQUES WHICH COULD BE USED IN CLASSROOM EVALUATION IN SCHOOLS

This list is in alphabetical order (and includes some duplication to allow for cross referencing):

Analytic memos These are short *periodic* analyses which consist of one's systematic thinking about the evidence one has collected.

Attainment tests These may be seen in the future, particularly with the new National Curriculum testing as *the* evaluation in schools. Hopefully, there will be some interpretation of these potentially simplistic evaluations by those not directly involved in the classroom, such as parents. As with many other areas of education, it may be up to teachers to educate others about the use of these results.

Audio recordings and transcripts Audio tape is easy to use, offers a permanent record which may be listened to repeatedly for analysis of classroom interactions. It is certainly *most* revealing for the first few times you hear your own voice. Transcription is time-consuming, but once again, it can be very revealing.

Case studies These are an in depth study of an element of the classroom. Many different types of evaluation are used in order to get as 'true' a picture as possible. Such studies may provide reference points for future as well as past work.

Checklists are often combined with questionnaires. These allow one to quantify people's observations, interpretations and attitudes and should be used as a means of checking against qualitative judgements.

Diaries of observations, feelings, reactions, interpretations, reflections, hunches, hypotheses and explanations. Diaries may be impressionistic or more systematic and analytical. They may also be by the teacher or (potentially more threateningly) by the pupils.

Discussions with one other person or with a group. Both have advantages and can be used at different times as needed.

Documents Although there are many documents within the school, they are not often used, to illuminate classroom practice. Some which may be useful are:

advisers, county inspectors or HMI reports
log books
pupils' worksheets
pupils' written or other work
school budgets
stock lists
syllabi
teaching plans
text books
timetables.

Field notes, drawings or plans These are 'rough' notes which may include a mass of information. They will certainly need analysis to sort out the useful and illuminating from the rest.

Interviewing It is very useful to use interviews for analysis. They can, however, be very time-consuming to obtain. Here are some which might be used:

By:	of:
teacher	pupils
critical friend	parents
colleague	teachers
	outsiders
	Head of Dept.
	Headteacher
	advisers
	inspectors (both county and HMI)

Lesson plans, notes or records may be used for evaluation a subsequent time. They may be used to link what was intended with what actually happened as is suggested by Stake's (1976) analysis.

Lesson profiles which, for example, may record teacher and pupil activity at ten minute intervals as opposed to the whole lesson.

Observation Direct observation may be used of pupil or teacher activity. It may therefore, be by the teacher or by somebody else. It may be for description or of observed systems of activity.

'Open house' classrooms for staff discussion.

Outside observer This is considered in greater depth in the Partnerships and Paired Observations section.

Participant observer The important and distinctive element of this type of evaluation is that it is not the main objective of the exercise. When teachers are working together they cannot help observing each other. These observations of each other's practice or of pupil behaviour make for interesting discussion.

Partnerships and Paired observations considered in depth following this list.

Photography Both prints and slides of classroom activity are most useful, not only as a record of the activity itself, but also for subsequent analysis.

Pupils' opinion and reactions This may require confidence on both the teacher's and the pupils' part that their views will be given and received in good faith. These opinions and reactions may be informally or formally obtained. Pupils' views may also be obtained from workbooks or any other work produced by the pupils.

Questionnaires can be useful for quantitative results. They are both time consuming and difficult to construct. Similarly it takes time to analyse the results. It is only therefore likely to be used for a largish evaluation.

Research and development 'interest groups' are groups of teachers who might share a particular interest or expertise which would benefit from further research. This might be developed for use in one or more schools.

The running commentary Here the teacher who is observing an individual or group should write down as much as possible of what he/she hears and observes. This is useful for short periods of observation of at least five minutes.

The shadow study This is as above, but the recorder is an observer from outside the classroom.

Sociometry is useful to evaluate the relationships within the classroom.

Staff workshops/conferences which concentrate on the practicalities of the management of learning.

Video recordings Potentially videotape is a most useful means of collecting both verbal and non-verbal information from within the classroom. Almost certainly, however, it requires another person to be present and may, initially, cause a distraction within the classroom. It does allow the teacher the opportunity for private self-evaluation and the chance to share this with others.

Work shadowing is perhaps more useful when looking at some of the management tasks in schools. Torrington and Weightman's sTAMp technique is particularly useful in this context in which *social, Technical*, i.e. teaching or any activity to do with children, *Administrative* work, i.e. that which could be completed by an intelligent sixteen year old, *Management* and *personal* activities are the categories used to analyse time spent during a day.

This list has been gained from the author's own experience together with information from the work of Elliott in *Facilitating Action Research in Schools, The Ford Teaching Project*, Holly & Southworth in *The Developing School*, May & Sigsworth in Murphy and Torrance *Evaluating Education: Issues and Methods*.

PARTNERSHIPS AND PAIRED OBSERVATIONS

One area was considered worthwhile for rather more detailed comments as it is such a potentially powerful technique, because, as Holly & Southworth in *The Developing School* write:

- observing the behaviour of other teachers may make a teacher aware of her own teaching
- it is a powerful learning experience in itself; it enables colleagues to share ideas
- teachers rarely see their peers teaching
- it helps to break down the 'psychological walls' between classrooms, thus eroding isolationism
- it can be non-threatening, informal and non-judgemental; it can provide an opportunity for 'mirroring' in terms of the partner collecting information for his/her colleague to use in self-evaluation
- within this kind of relationship, team spirit, trust and collaboration can develop over time
- it is both child-focused and teacher-focused; indeed it is **learning-focused**
- it provides stimulation arising from discussion, reflection, analysis and collaborative action.

May & Sigsworth in Murphy and Torrance *Evaluating Education: Issues and Methods* give the benefits of the partnership approach to in-service activity as follows:

- It offers the school the professional satisfaction, even excitement, of conducting an inquiry into aspects of their own teaching.
- It counters the sense of isolation often felt by teachers in schools where travel problems make it difficult for them to get to after-school in-service meetings held at a distance.
- It offers a relationship with someone outside the teacher's everyday professional group. This can be important both in helping the teacher to see that what he or she is doing is worthwhile and in translating thought into action.

The outside partner offers 'a second pair of eyes'. She gathers evidence through observation to illuminate a problem or concern that the teacher has identified as worth exploring. Through discussion, the outsider helps to analyse and interpret the evidence, thus deepening the teacher's understanding of some aspect of his or her teaching.

Holly & Southworth in *The Developing School* continue that as evaluations were exchanged, teachers developed more respect for the ability of their colleagues to make sound judgements and were more willing to be evaluated. By doing evaluation, they themselves became more evaluative. The evaluation work, conducted in partnerships, consisted of seven interrelated steps:

- **Finding a partner**: it proved important to build in friendship and voluntaryism as two 'principles of procedure' as the 'climate' of the pairing revolving around the need for trust, respect, honesty, and supportiveness was crucial.
- **Selecting evaluation criteria**—or performance indicators.
- **Self-assessment (based on the chosen criteria).**
- **Pupil assessment** i.e. an evaluation of the teacher by the pupils.
- **Paired observations**, based on an exchange deal within the pairing and using the chosen criteria.
- **Conferencing**, involving feedback and practical suggestions and the initiation of an 'improvement plan'.
- **Improvement plans** to be finalised and implemented.

A 'contract' may need to be agreed. This may have the following:

- **Focus of observation**: to be chosen by the teacher and discussed until the outsider feels that the brief is understood and that it is clearly enough articulated to shape the observation. The focus may be refined or redefined by the teacher as appropriate.

- **Method of observation**: to be discussed by the two partners in terms of suitability to the chosen focus and any constraints of the classroom situation. The method may be refined or modified, as appropriate, during the course of the partnership.

- **Observational record**: to consist of non-judgemental notes made by the outsider, preferably in a carbon copy notebook so that sets of notes are immediately available for both the teacher and the outsider to study.

- **Post-observation discussion**: to be conducted as soon as possible after the observation. The outsider has the responsibility for making a summary of this discussion so that it is possible for both partners to recall, at their next meeting, where they got to in their analysis and interpretation of the data presented in the observational record.

- **Formative or summative discussion of procedures**: at any stage during the partnership, either partner should be free to take the initiative in calling for a review of the way that the partnership is working.

- **Confidentiality**: the outsider guarantees to regard the observations, the observational records, and the discussions and summaries of discussion as confidential information.

Outside partners have advantages over inside teacher colleague partners for the following reasons:

- they are neutral professionals
- the outsider is coming in to the school to show that the teacher is not isolated
- the teacher is more in touch with the world outside her own classroom
- teachers sometimes have no sense of how their work compares with work in other schools
- teachers may think they are idiosyncratic, failing, old-fashioned, and so on
- the outsider may serve to extend the teacher's thinking.

PROBLEMS INVOLVED WITH CLASSROOM BASED EVALUATION

TIME

The first and main problem with all these techniques is that they take time. In the present, post-ERA, time is precious. There is a variety of teaching to be completed and with the introduction of the National Curriculum and testing any classroom evaluation has to be *seen* as worthwhile to the teacher as an individual. If this is not perceived to be so then it will have little value.

ENTHUSIASM AND EFFORT

Enthusiasm and effort is needed as well as the perseverance to complete a planned evaluation. It is encouraging to note that in research it was found that teachers were 'excited' by classroom evaluation.

TECHNICAL PROBLEMS

There may be technical problems with such areas as:

- sampling
- reliability
- distortion of the results.

Hopefully these are likely to be recognised and allowed for in any evaluation.

ACTION PLANS

Sometimes it is not easy to see what action to take even when a teacher has a deeper understanding of the situation through classroom evaluation. In these circumstances it may be worth asking these questions:

- What do I **need** to do?
- What am I **willing** to do?
- What **will** I do?

and subsequently:

- Whom can I ask for help?
- Whom do I trust to ensure my progress?

FINDING THE RIGHT PERSON TO HELP

Finding the right person to help is not an easy task. In the first instance the teacher needs to be willing to enter a partnership. What are the qualities needed in a partner? These might be some of the qualities needed:

- familiarity with age group being taught
- familiarity with subject area being taught
- experience of classrooms
- sensitivity
- confidentiality
- capacity to be unobtrusive.

In small schools an outsider coming in to a small group which is already open and easy could restrict the freedom of internal talk and cause friction.

The teacher needs to be confident
Finally the teacher needs the confidence to try out new activities and even more confidence to realise that she might fail to live up to her own expectations. Teachers are not used to others in the classroom who are not either 'learner' teachers or authority figures so it is sometimes difficult for teachers to see a visitor as a 'research partner'. What is being suggested here needs to be seen as research into what is going on in the classroom, how to evaluate it and the action to take to make learning even better for the pupils.

MANAGEMENT ISSUES

Action-research is pitted against the 'bureaucratic understanding' of those employed to promote institutional constraints on individual 'freedom', i.e. school managers. Action-research, according to this argument, may be seen as a political, destabilising force; the managed versus the managers. What, then, is the management style conducive to evaluation and one which will foster and not undermine staff commitment to the various schemes which have been suggested in this and other chapters?

The Developing School, put forward by Reid, Hopkins and Holly, has a capability for being innovative. But innovations are introduced in a certain, developmental, style. Strengths are identified and retained; other areas in need of priority attention are investigated. The aim is to synthesise the best of the old with the best of the new. The responsibility for this work should be grounded in the body of the staff. The Developing School rests on staff development and is energised by the supportiveness of staff collaboration within school based INSET.

What is crucial is that the Developing School demands to be 'managed' in a certain style—a style which, ideally, should reflect the nuances of the management of learning at classroom level. School management should help teachers to learn how to facilitate learning. The conducive style should be as follows:

- Participative and consultative. All staff should be **involved** —both ideologically and in terms of the consequent practice in the classroom.

- Invoking and facilitating of staff commitment and ownership.

- Supportive, collaborative and collegial; it should provide an enabling framework.

- Preoccupied with the orchestration of talent and expertise that is the staff. This involves the identification of personal strengths within a team approach. It also involves the fostering of responsibility across the staff. It is appropriate for the developing primary school to include this in the School Development Plan as required following the 1988 Education Act.

- Keenly aware of the importance and effectiveness of staff relationships and the climate of the school. Cultural values and norms lie at the heart of this climate. Thus openness, trust, a preparedness to face risk and ambiguity, a positive attitude to criticism, etc., may well be vital 'principles of procedure' for the Developing School.

If evaluation and its management is to belong to the teachers then it needs to be internalised. This will mean the provision of process guidelines which are action documents as enabling, flexible frameworks as a part of the School Development Plans.

4
Action

Evaluation is not a worthwhile activity unless it includes **ACTION**. This chapter is concerned with the *management* of this most important aspect of evaluation and helps to give the management techniques to achieve the evaluation cycle of your school in your own way. Items which have been included elsewhere in the book are often repeated within this context in this chapter.

Evaluation is not a single activity, but a series of activities which must be undertaken in sequence if the whole is to be successful. They have been presented as a list to emphasise the sequentiality of the process. These activities are:

A DETAILED EVALUATION CYCLE

- **DEVELOPING A TEAM**
  Who can help?

- **THE SCHOOL ENVIRONMENT**
  What are our beliefs?
  What is the situation, in general?
  Where do we want to be?
  The Context for the Audit
  The aims and values of the school
  Policies and initiatives from central government and the LEA
  Trends, changes in parents' attitudes
  Recent or anticipated competitor actions
  Other views and perspectives
  The School Development Plan (SDP)

- **EVALUATION OR AUDIT**
  What is the situation, here?
  What is happening now?
  What is *really* happening now?
  The Content of the Audit
  RESEARCH and Collection of information
  ANALYSIS of the information

- **PRODUCTION OF AN IMPLEMENTATION PLAN**
  STRATEGY—What do we want to do about it?
  Definition of aims
  What methods are we going to use?
  Resources
  Time
  OBJECTIVES—How are we going to go about it?
  Developing objectives
  Establishing priorities
  OPERATIONAL PROGRAMMES—What are our Action Plans?
  Production of Action Plans and their approval

- **IMPLEMENTATION**
  Doing it!
  Communication
  Written documents
  Face to face communications

- **MONITORING AND EVALUATION**
  How did we get on?
  QUALITY CONTROL
  Performance indicators

It is further suggested that the process of evaluation is cyclic or spiral in nature as opposed to linear for the evaluation items link strongly with the implementation. This is shown in diagrammatic form on the following page.

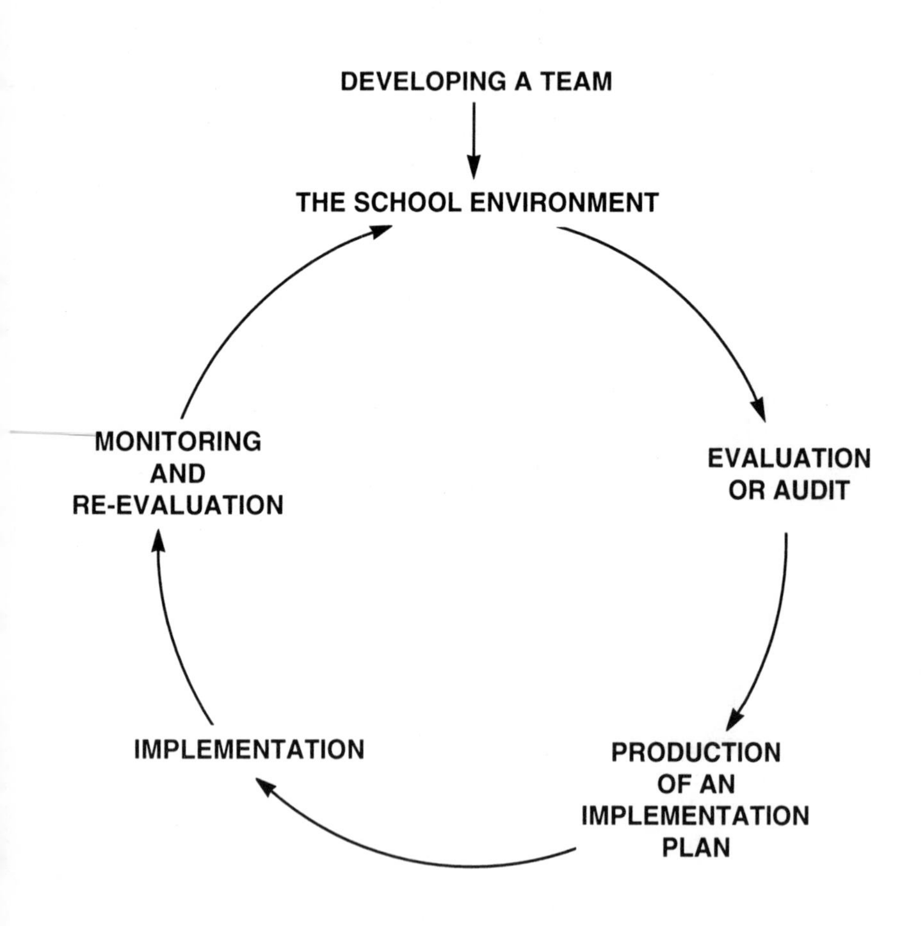

THE EVALUATION CYCLE

DEVELOPING A TEAM

Neither the management nor the implementation of the evaluation of the school can be achieved by one person. It is the kind of task that needs a small *team* of people to work together. There are two reasons for having a team. The first is that by sharing out the various tasks amongst a group it will lighten the load on any one person. The second reason is that by having a group there is likely to be a widening of ideas, expertise and viewpoints.

It is suggested that a senior member of staff should be responsible for the managing of the evaluation of the school. This may or may not be the Headteacher, but it certainly should be somebody who has influence within the school and also somebody who is interested in doing the task. This person should work closely with the Head.

The small team could include governors or parents with the relevant expertise or interest, as well as teachers. The first, of many, activities is to list those people who *could* help, together with what they have to offer in order. Try to be as creative and divergent in your thinking to include as many people as possible. This may include those from outside as well as inside the school. Having listed the possible people, the next stage is to choose those who are most likely to build into the right team.

Having built the team, it is suggested that each of the elements in the cycle is taken in turn.

THE SCHOOL ENVIRONMENT

This section is in answer to such questions as:

- What are our beliefs?
- What is the situation, in general?
- Where do we want to be?

What are our beliefs?

It is important that **everything** that we do in the school is set firmly in what we believe. It is not by chance, therefore, that the first of the points to be considered in the context of any evaluation is the aims and values of the school as these should be firmly kept in the front of our minds throughout any evaluation.

What is the situation, in general?
Our school cannot be considered separately, hence the reasons for considering the views of central government, the LEA, parents and other schools in the area.

Where do we want to be?
The answer to this question of 'Where do we want to be in one year, two years, three years, five years . . . ?' should be set within the School Development Plan as any evaluation in the school should be considered within this context.

The Context for the Audit
Any evaluation of the school as a whole or any aspect of it, including its planning and implementation needs to be set within:

- the aims and values of the school
- policies and initiatives from central government and the LEA
- trends, changes in parents' attitudes
- recent or anticipated competitor actions
- other views and perspectives
- the School Development Plan (SDP).

The aims and values of the school
Evaluation of the school needs to be set within the aims and values of the school as a whole and not considered in isolation. If these aims and values are not already written down in a form which can be used in this context it may be necessary to start by devising a **MISSION STATEMENT** of what the school **does** aim to do. The advantage of a school mission statement is that **everything** which happens within the school can then be aimed at achieving this purpose. Certainly the evaluation of the school should reflect the values of the school as a whole. Examples of this might be if the school sees itself as an academic institution, with strict discipline and uniform, the evaluation should reflect this not only in its content, but also its style. In contrast the school may be one which prides itself on being a caring, relaxed place where learning is only a part of the experience of the children. In this case the style of evaluation will be totally different.

Policies and initiatives from central government and the LEA
Government policies such as the introduction of the National

Curriculum and its assessment and LEA policies on open enrolment cannot be ignored. Which are the most important for *your* school? How do you see your school fitting in to the national scene and that of the Local Education Authority? Is there a new initiative which has to be included in the curriculum? Is staffing, or lack of it, an issue? Is there a new housing estate being built near you? Are they building a new school? What are the trends in population, both in general and also that of school age? The school cannot isolate itself from what is happening in the rest of the area and needs to consider not only how this is affecting the school now, but also in the near future, say in the next year, and also the more distant future, say three or five years' time.

Trends, changes in parents' attitudes

What are the trends in your area concerning all the schools? Are these trends which are easy or difficult to change? Which of these trends *can* you change and which cannot be changed, so are not worth the time and effort attempting to do so? The answers to these and many other questions concerning the trends in your area need to be considered.

What are the changes in parents' attitudes which are important in your area? For example are the parents' attitudes changing towards or away from state education in your area? Perhaps this is something on which you could work collectively to change with other schools near you, if it is too large a project to be considered by a single school.

Recent or anticipated competitor actions

Once more, what are other schools in your area doing? If you started an evaluation of your school now, would you be in the lead? Or is the converse true – everybody else is well on the way and you have to catch up? Can you afford *not* to evaluate your school when everybody else is doing so? As before you should consider not only what is happening now, but also what might happen in the near and distant future.

Other views and perspectives

What other views might be taken into consideration? What are the views of the governors, parents, even pupils as well as teachers on all of the above points and on the evaluation on which you are about to embark? Does it *matter* what others think?

The School Development Plan (SDP)

This is now an integral part of the management of the school. It should be a working document which is in constant use, therefore any evaluation should be included with this overall plan. This may have repercussions as far as reporting, control, confidentiality and involvement of parents and governors. So it may be that small evaluations in which teachers may be sensitive to these issues should *not* be included in the SDP.

EVALUATION OR AUDIT

This section attempts to answer the questions:

- What is the situation, here?
- What is happening now?
- What is *really* happening now?

This evaluation needs to be as dispassionate and impersonal as possible. It is very easy to *think* that we know what is happening, without seeking *evidence* to support our views.

The Content of the Audit

This has two parts:

- RESEARCH and COLLECTION of information
- ANALYSIS of the information

RESEARCH AND COLLECTION OF INFORMATION

Wherever possible try to accumulate both QUANTITATIVE and QUALITATIVE information. Quantitative information is that which can be counted, added up and quantified whereas qualitative information is that which, although it cannot be counted, is valuable because it contains our feelings about the situation.

Collect appropriate information by using one or more of the techniques suggested in chapters two or three of this book.

An evaluation or audit needs to be:

- Comprehensive
- Systematic
- Objective
- Periodic.

Comprehensive
The evaluation or audit needs to be comprehensive in that it covers the whole of the organisation or a part of it and not just those areas which are causing concern. It should be as wide ranging as possible in the areas which are investigated and not narrow and inward looking. It is also worth mentioning that depending on the available budget and time constraints, the information gathering effort should be reliable.

Systematic
The evaluation should be systematic. In this and other sections it is intended to help the reader by giving the systematic process to be followed and also a variety of activities to be completed.

Objective
It is all too easy to make the evaluation a cosy, self-congratulating process. It is suggested here that it should be as rigorous as possible and that the audit should be as objective as possible by using governors, parents and others from outside the school if it is thought that this will help.

Periodic
Although many schools have been undertaking evaluations of one sort or another for many years it is suggested that evaluation is not a 'one off', but a regular, repeated activity. It needs to be regularly updated as it is easy for the information to get out of date quite quickly. It should be part of a plan and not be completed only when something untoward crops up.

ANALYSIS OF THE INFORMATION

The educational world is full of data which have been collected and then nothing further has happened. Analysis is a time-consuming and potentially expensive activity. It can be carried out most effectively, and cheaply, if the analysis stage is considered and thought through before the collection is made.

Unprocessed data are of little value to management or teaching staff. A superficial look through a set of questionnaires will not suffice if the best use is to be made of the data. Properly analysed, information should be fed back to teaching and management staff as appropriate.

It is not intended to go into detail about the analysis of

information in this book, but it is worthwhile to suggest that some of the following might be considered.

Quantitative data
Production of:

- tally charts
- graphs: column, line or pie as appropriate
- tables of information.

Qualitative data
This is often better done using a word processor and might include:

- typing in of raw data
- collecting similar comments together under appropriate headings
- re-ordering of the comments within these headings
- making a synopsis of the comments
- listing the main points made.

The key role for professional staff in such an evaluation lies in bridging the gap between the information and the action which results from it. How to achieve this action will be considered in later stages. Staff should not merely *react* to the views expressed and automatically make changes suggested by the parents, children or anybody else. School teaching and management staff must *interpret* the information produced by the above stages and make professional decisions which are best for the school in the short, medium and long term. It is on their own judgement that they must ultimately rely.

PRODUCTION OF AN IMPLEMENTATION PLAN

This section will consider the production of an implementation plan and will involve:

- **STRATEGY**—What do we want to do about it?
  Definition of aims
  Methods
  Resources
  Time.

- **OBJECTIVES**—How are we going to go about it?
  Developing objectives
  Establishing priorities.

- **OPERATIONAL PROGRAMMES**—What are our Action plans?
  Production of Action Plans and their approval.

STRATEGY
This section on strategy is that having done an evaluation, what do we want to **do** about it? There is little point in carrying out an evaluation if no action in one form or another is going to result from it!

Definition of aims
In terms of strategy, it would seem the first task is to decide what it is we are trying to achieve. This should link back very strongly to the whole **purpose** of the evaluation. These aims are likely to be 'global' terms. What is the desired outcome of the whole evaluation process? It could be an ongoing and comprehensive evaluation of the whole school or an evaluation of the introduction of the National Curriculum. Or more specifically, an evaluation of the role of the Deputy Head or the use of out of school time for extra-curricular activities. There may be a whole series of aims. Planning in education is as much concerned with what is possible as with what is desirable.

An alternative method is to list the main differences between your beliefs and where you want to be, and where you are now. You will then need to plan the route between these two positions and the steps to help you progress from one to the other.

What methods are we going to use?
Identify as many methods or activities as possible that *could* be used to implement the findings of the evaluation. Be as creative as possible at this stage. This is another area where it helps to have a team of people involved as they are likely to have more ideas than one person. Some of these may already be used, some may be new to your school.

Resources

The strategy will need to include thoughts about the resources which are **needed** and perhaps more important the resources which are **available.** One of the problems here may be that there is no precedent for the use of resources in this fashion. It may be that there has never been a budget for this area of development or improvement in the past, so it may be difficult to determine one the future. Quality in education does not always mean an increase in costs or resources; sometimes it means a change in attitudes or a *re*-allocation of resources.

Time

Time is a resource worth considering here. Not only the time which it is **desirable** to spend on the improvement or change, but also the time which the Head, staff and others are **prepared** to spend. The two may not be the same.

What is the time frame of your improvement programme? What do you plan to do this year, this term?

Having sorted out in principle what you might wish to do in broad brush strokes, the next stage is the rather more detailed one of how we are going to go about it.

OBJECTIVES

Developing objectives

Once improvement activities are selected, determine the objectives to be accomplished. Objectives should be SMART and MAC FEW OI!, as described earlier in this book. These objectives should be decided by the senior management team in conjunction with staff, governors and also parents and the LEA if appropriate.

The education manager will need to examine what could help and hinder the plan and may need to decide on the differing tactics which may need to be employed with these very differing groups in order to reach consensus.

Establish your priorities

Having decided on the objectives, these should be prioritised. This should involve not only deciding which are the most **important** activities, but also the **order** in which they should be completed. The staff in particular should have a major role to play here as it is likely they will be the main, but not the only, people involved in the implementation of any scheme. Everybody should now know what they are trying to achieve and should work single-mindedly towards success.

OPERATIONAL PROGRAMMES

Production of Action Plans

An ACTION PLAN should include, as described earlier in this book:

WHO should do **WHAT** by **WHEN?**

That is, a *NAMED PERSON* to complete a *SPECIFIC ACTIVITY* within an agreed *TIME.*

This will be a detailed schedule of what is to be completed this term, this month and this week as opposed to this year.

It is important to progress through the stages of STRATEGY, OBJECTIVES and ACTION PLAN as they are separate stages in which the first is concerned with general principles, the second with the tactics and finally the small detail in the Action Plan. Each of the first two stages will need consultation with staff and governors before they are made public. The final stage is to obtain the resource needed and get the programme under way. Make frequent checks to be sure the approach is on the right track.

In summary then a plan must:

- explain the situation, both present and future
- specify results that are expected
- be explicit
- be intelligible to all concerned
- identify the resources that will be needed to carry out the planned actions
- describe the actions that are to take place and who is responsible for implementing them
- permit monitoring the ensuing actions and results
- Although written, also be capable of accepting change.

The manager might also need to think about the major **obstacles** to adopting this plan and consider anything which could **help** or **hinder** the implementation plan.

Although on balance these techniques are of potential use to the education manager as a tool for analysis, they would have to be accepted into a school's organisational culture for wider application.

Planning is a necessary managerial activity that is often neglected in schools. It is necessary to emphasise the importance of balance between a time-consuming systematic approach to planning and no planning at all.

IMPLEMENTATION

Having looked at your beliefs, analysed the environment in general and in particular, conducted an evaluation or audit and produced an Action Plan, it is now time to stop talking and **DO** something. It is important to ensure that the action being done is that which was agreed upon and which is intended. It is all about managing the process itself – managing the journey towards completing the improvement. It is about motivation and is often concerned as much with communication as with action. This communication will normally be in the form of:

- written documents
- face to face communications.

The previous stage was concerned with producing a series of written working documents and these are very important. It is more likely, however, that the second of these, face to face communications, will be more effective at changing people's views about the school and education in general. Yet much of the effort in schools seems to be on the former. In this section, **BOTH** are considered to be vital.

Internal communication often creates the greatest of problems and sometimes suffers from the greatest neglect. It is assumed because it was discussed at a staff meeting and agreed at that time, then it will all happen as planned. Unfortunately this is unlikely to be true.

The school should organise an effective internal communications programme because:

- the school will never reach its objectives unless all those involved with the school understand what the objectives are

- everybody needs to know their individual role in helping reach those objectives
- members of the school feel a greater sense of ownership when they *are* involved
- members of staff, both teaching and non-teaching have knowledge and skills that can be tapped to make the school more effective. Working in partnership can lead to a sense of teamwork, where the staff as a whole becomes greater than the sum of its individual parts
- the right hand must know what the left hand is doing.

Considering that face to face communication is most influential, those managing the school must talk to all those concerned with the implementation plan whilst that implementation is happening. This is not only **management by walking about** (MBWA), but commenting on what is going on, constantly encouraging and helping where possible. Managers should try to catch members of staff doing things **right** and then praise them for it, rather than catch people doing things wrong and having to correct or reprimand them.

It makes sense for the Head to consider every member of the staff, both teaching and non-teaching, that is *all* those who work in the school, as important members of the school team. They should be kept informed of all the major issues facing the school— not just those in their specific area of responsibility— and should be made to feel that they are a valued part of the school 'family'. The importance of cultivating that 'family feeling' cannot be overstated. Open, honest, two-way communication is the bulwark of high morale and is the key to motivated staff. A sense of community results from the sharing of common information, common feelings, and common objectives. That sense of community can exist within the staff when all feel informed, when they feel involved and when they feel their ideas are heard.

All of the previous paragraph is also true for the governors, parents and pupils. Everybody should be involved, wherever possible, in making improvements work. It may even be necessary to involve a wider audience, if this is appropriate, and this might include non-parents, feeder schools, local industry, as well as District and County Councillors and even Members of Parliament. Open Days where visitors see pupils actually at work in their classrooms and putting the improvements into practice may even be considered.

MONITORING AND EVALUATION

This section is not only in answer to the question 'How *did* we get on?', but also to the question 'How *are* we getting on?' monitoring is about making adjustments to the plan, both small and large. It is about re-allocation of resources. It is about quality control. There is a sub-cycle of the main cycle which involves a constant monitoring, *re*-planning, *re*-implementation, followed by more monitoring, more planning, more implementation and so on.

There are two reasons for the necessity to have a monitoring and evaluation programme:

- Were the improvements made, did we carry out the action?
- To compare the implementation of the plan with what actually happened and is continuing to happen.

This section needs to be:

- comprehensive
- systematic
- objective
- periodic.

and will involve:

- collection of information and
- analysis of the information.

This similarity is not accidental and allows for this to be used as the beginning of the second cycle. As before the information may be collected by the most appropriate methods and the information used, perhaps, to produce a database for reference in the future.

As suggested earlier, indicators show up a particular success or possible problem. This indication can be followed up with a series of one-to-one interviews in order to obtain further, more detailed information. Having done this a report needs to be prepared summarising and analysing the points made in the interviews.

This report may help in the evaluation of the problem and it may help to identify whether it is viewed as an issue connected with:

- communication
- resources
- staff development
- the evaluation process itself.

This enables the 'right' re-planning or re-implementation to be adopted.

Quality monitoring allows schools to review their academic and other services **taking a client-centred perspective**. This will not be considered here, but readers may like to refer to *Marketing the Primary School* by the same author for further information on this aspect of evaluation.

In order to assist the reader there follows an example of an evaluation cycle, together with a number of activities.

A CURRICULUM PLAN—EXAMPLE

Primary education has, in recent years, become appreciably more complex: the increasing demands for the teaching of science and technology and new approaches to learning reading and writing are but two examples. These demands have, in turn, led to changes in the teaching approaches in some schools; changes designed to improve the match between teaching and learning and to offer an increasing range of opportunities to pupils.

Changes have thus been taking place on a gradual basis over a period of time, but often in a patchy and *ad hoc* manner. The introduction of the National Curriculum was intended not only to build on and enhance this process of change, but also to accelerate the use of the best practice across the entire system. The major difference is that the National Curriculum (which is statutory) is non-negotiable as a framework for every school and as an entitlement for all pupils.

As with other changes gradually introduced over the last few years the successful introduction and implementation of the National Curriculum will depend on effective planning.

A STEP BY STEP APPROACH TO CURRICULUM PLANNING FROM A WHOLE SCHOOL PRESPECTIVE

THE SCHOOL ENVIRONMENT

Consider the curriculum the school will offer
This must include:

the core subjects:	English
	Mathematics
	Science
the other foundation subjects:	History
	Geography
	Music
	Art
	Physical Education
	Religious Education
	Technology.

Examine the LEA curriculum statements
With governors, agree on any modifications desired.

Set the basic curriculum subjects in the context of the whole curriculum of the school
By examining current policies or initiating new policies to include:

- multi-cultural education
- equal opportunities
- personal and social education including cross-curricular themes such as: health education
  environmental education
  economic and industrial understanding
- special educational needs
- information technology.

These dimensions should be woven throughout the life and work of the school, in every area of the curriculum and be addressed by every teacher. It is essential that there is a common *school* viewpoint which will guarantee a consistent approach.

CARRY OUT A CURRICULUM AUDIT

What is happening now?
What does the curriculum consist of at present?
What are its strengths?
What are its weaknesses?
How does the curriculum compare with the requirements of the National Curriculum Attainment Targets and Programmes of Study in foundation subjects?
What are the gaps?
What action is needed to fill them?

*What is **really** happening now?*
What dispassionate evidence is there?
Is an outside view needed? e.g. other Heads (Critical Colleagues), LEA advisers, HMI reports.
There is a need for all involved in planning to be honest and open.

What do we need to do next?
This is not a journey into the unknown as much is already being done, albeit unevenly and sporadically.
It is suggested that we *manage and build on what we are doing already*.

ANALYSE THE USE OF TIME

This is the whole time available for children to learn.
What do we *have* to do?
What restrictions are there on using this time for formal curriculum delivery? e.g. assembly, registration, unforeseen accidents/incidents, movement around the school, changing from one activity to another.
Do all staff need to go to assemblies?
How much time is left for the core and other foundation subjects?
Schools need to bear in mind the requirement that the core and other foundation subjects are to be taught for a 'reasonable time'.
What comprises a 'reasonable time' is not defined in the ERA.
Schools must be able to demonstrate that provision is made for every subject of the National Curriculum to receive 'worthwhile' study by each pupil during each Key Stage.
What do we understand by 'reasonable' and 'worthwhile'?
HMI found 82% of time was being given to core subjects and the rest to foundation subjects, if they were done at all.
How is time used at the present?

How do you make decisions about how time is spent now?
There is a need to **prioritise**.
Is it necessary to establish **new** priorities in the use of time?
How will this be done?
The most likely question, as the first stages of the National Curriculum are put into place, will be,

- How do we find the time?

The answer must lie in being willing to question all existing practice and assumptions.

TIME IS A CREATIVE CURRICULUM MANAGEMENT TOOL

DECIDE ON THE ACQUISITION AND DEPLOYMENT OF RESOURCES
This will include both human and material resources and will need frequent, regular review and re-assessment of priorities.

AGREE ON WAYS OF INFORMING PUPILS, PARENTS AND GOVERNORS ABOUT PLANNED CURRICULUM PROVISION

Planning needs to be at three levels:

- whole school
- class
- individual pupil.

For each level, planning needs to be considered in the context of:

- short-term (say up to a term)
- medium-term (say up to a year)
- long-term (say up to three years).

To be effective planning needs to respond to change.

ESTABLISH A SCHOOL CURRICULUM DEVELOPMENT PLAN

This will need to address the changes and modifications that need to be made to implement the National Curriculum and will be based on the 'curriculum audit'. The plan needs to consider both curriculum and organisational changes, including Local Management of Schools (LMS). It will address these questions:

Where are we now?

Where do we need to get to?

How much time have we got to get there?

How do we do it?

Who will do it?

The aim is to establish a whole school plan within which every teacher must work

SOME ADDITIONAL CONSIDERATIONS ON PRIMARY CURRICULUM DELIVERY

Curriculum planning in primary schools

- Schools should plan the needs of individual pupils *then* look at styles of presenting this and *not the other way round*

- Programmes of Study are important to make decisions

- Do not start with Topic Webs and then try to 'shoe-horn' the attainment targets in, but look at the **subjects** and then look for **links** or **common threads**

- Keep it simple

- Use the same management strategies over *years* not months.

MAJOR AREAS TO TAKE ON BOARD

Management issues

(Whole school approach—not individual teachers)
Planning and management *skills*
Working as a member of a team
How to contribute to a team

Classroom organisation

(Look at grouping of children)
How do we cope with different levels?
How are we doing it now?
What strategies are in use now?

Common thread issues

Coherent and rational strategies
Planning of curriculum delivery

Knowledge base of teachers

e.g. Science, Technology, History
Understanding of Programmes of Study and Key Stages for all the subject areas and then looking at how to deliver them.

Problems and issues

ACHIEVABILITY: What we are really doing at the present i.e. using CONCRETE, FIRST HAND EXPERIENCES *but* it **MUST BE IN A PLANNED FRAMEWORK** with progression and continuity.

We must then **communicate** to parents what we do in the school.

ACTIVITIES

Some of the questions which have been asked in this section are now presented in a form which may make it easier for those doing these activities to use.

DEVELOPING A TEAM

Who should be responsible for the implementation plan?

LIST THOSE PEOPLE WHO COULD HELP

	Names	What they have to offer
Staff		
Governors		
Parents		
Others		

SCHOOL ENVIRONMENT

THE CONTEXT FOR THE AUDIT

The aims and values of the school

What are the main aims of the school?

What are the values which the school thinks are important?

Mission Statement

Devise a Mission Statement for the school.

A Mission Statement must include the main aims and purposes of the school in no more than 25 words. Ideally this is a group activity for all the staff.

SCHOOL ENVIRONMENT

THE CONTEXT FOR THE AUDIT

Policies and initiatives from Central Government and the LEA
What are the main policies and initiatives from central government which you are trying to adopt at the present time?

What are the main policies and initiatives from the LEA which you are trying to adopt at the present time?

Trends
What are the trends in your area which you need to consider?

Go through this list and put a star beside those about which you can do nothing.

Changes in parents' attitudes
What are the changes in parents' attitudes which are important in your area?

Recent or anticipated competitor actions
What are the recent or anticipated actions being made by your competitors?

Other views and perspectives
What other views and perspectives need to be considered in your school?

COST OF COLLECTING INFORMATION

In order to assist in the collection of data, it sometimes helps to decide exactly what data you require and how costly it might be to find. That is what this matrix is designed to do.

Column 1	*Column 2*	*Column 3*	*Column 4*	*Column 5*
Questions	Information required	Likely sources of information	Accessibility of information	Cost of information

Some of the questions which have been mentioned previously may be put in Column 1.

Having completed that column, complete the others.

Column 4 is scored 0 = not available
1 = access very difficult
2 = needs some effort
3 = readily available

Column 5 is scored 1 = very expensive
2 = significant costs
3 = low/no costs

This information may be summarised on one sheet:

Questions	Information Inaccessible and costly	Information Inaccessible not costly	Information Accessible and costly	Information Accessible not costly	Recommendations

PRODUCTION OF AN IMPLEMENTATION PLAN STRATEGY

Definition Of Aims

What is the desired outcome?

What is planned this year?

What is planned this term?

What methods are to be used?

What resources are needed?

What resources are available?

What time is it desirable to spend?

What time are you prepared to spend?

PRODUCTION OF AN IMPLEMENTATION PLAN OBJECTIVES

Objectives should be:

SMART

- **S**pecific
- **M**easurable—this is the most important point
- **A**ttainable
- **R**ealistic
- **T**ime constrained.

MAC FEW OI!

- **M**easurable within **A**ny **C**onstraints
- **A**chievable
- **C**hallenging

Few in number

- **F**lexible
- **E**asily
- **W**ritten

OI! Do It Now!

- **O**rganisational
- **I**ndividual

DEVELOPING OBJECTIVES

What are your objectives for this **year**?

What are your objectives for this **term**?

What are your objectives for this **month**?

What are your objectives for this **week**?

ESTABLISH PRIORITIES

What are your priorities? Take another look at your objectives and then number them in order of priority.

PRODUCTION OF AN IMPLEMENTATION PLAN OPERATIONAL PROGRAMMES

An **ACTION PLAN** should include:

WHO should do **WHAT** by **WHEN**

Production of Action Plans

This will be a detailed schedule of what is to be completed.

NAMED PERSON	to complete **SPECIFIC ACTIVITY**	within an agreed **TIME**

EVALUATION: DID WE DO WHAT WE PLANNED?

The object of this valuation is to compare the *implementation* of the plan with what actually happened.

Which of the activities we planned, did we **complete?**

Which of the activities we planned, did we **not complete?**

Why did we not complete them?

Lack of effort?

Lack of time?

Lack of resources?

Other reasons?

5
Conclusion

Birnbaum in his article *Monitoring and evaluation in the new era* in the *Education* magazine of 25 August 1989 gives seven main criteria to be applied to any arrangements and procedures for monitoring and evaluation. These would seem to sum up the processes which have been included in this book. The seven criteria are:

- **They must be credible**
  i.e. all involved must have confidence in the process and outcomes.
- **The outcomes must be valuable to all parties**
  e.g. they should help to enhance teaching and learning.
- **They must be cost-effective**
  i.e. the time and resources spent on each exercise must be justified by the outcome.
- **The evidence collected must be reliable**
  i.e. the same evidence would have been collected by any other competent enquirer.
- **The judgements made must be valid**
  i.e. they must be adequately supported by the evidence.
- **The process should be verifiable**
  i.e. all the evidence should be clear, and the reasons for the judgements made should be articulated.
- **The lessons from the process should be transferable**
  e.g. elements of good practice should be described in a way that others can learn from them.

FINALLY

A few final comments on evaluation in general:

- Be prepared for disappointments, but also expect a few pleasant surprises.
- Avoid any temptation to be outraged. Teachers are adults who have given their consent to the evaluation.
- Frequency—not too often, but don't forget it altogether.
- Anticipation is often as valuable as the activity itself.
- It is usually more successful if it is done in private.
- Talk about it openly.
- Work within established relationships, but be adventurous.
- Don't rely too much on norms or averages.

Glossary

Accountability in the strict sense to one's employers or political masters (contractual accountability).

Accountability is answerability to one's clients, i.e. parents and pupils (moral accountability).

Accountability is responsibility to oneself and one's colleagues (professional accountability).

Appraisal emphasises the forming of qualitative judgements about an activity, a person or an organisation. It is not normally, however, used in this general way in school as it is now assumed to be connected with personal performance.

Assessment implies the use of measurement and/or grading based on known criteria. It is therefore usually quantitative, precise and acceptable when used in relation to children but once again it may have slightly negative connotations when linked with teachers.

CERI Centre for Educational Research and Innovation.

DION Diagnosing Individual and Organisational Needs.

DIY Do It Yourself.

Evaluation is seen as a general term to describe any activity within the school where the quality of what is happening or what we are trying to do is the subject. This may or may not be systematic.

Formal impersonal, external, accurate, valid, credible.

Formative developmental, diagnostic concerning continuous assessment and professional development.

GRIDS Guidelines for Review and Internal Development in Schools.

HMI Her Majesty's Inspectorate.

IMTEC/SDG International Movements Towards Educational Change/School Development Guide.
ILEA Inner London Education Authority.
Informal personal, internal.
INSET In-Service Education for Teachers.
ISIP The International School Improvement Project.
LEA Local Education Authority is the organisation which manages schools within a county or metropolitan borough.
LMS Local Management of Schools is a scheme by which schools have control over their own budgets.
Objective concerned with measurement and 'facts'.
OECD Organisation for Economic Co-operation and Development.
OFSTED Office for STandards in EDucation.
Qualitative a method of evaluation which concentrates on the qualities and does not include measurement.
Quantitative quantity measurement in one form or another.
Review indicates a retrospective activity and implies the collection and examination of evidence and information.
SBR School Based Review.
School Improvement is a systematic, sustained effort aimed at change in learning conditions and other related internal conditions in one or more schools, with the ultimate aim of accomplishing educational goals more effectively.
SDP School Development Plan is a plan for the whole school which has been a requirement of the 1988 Education Act.
Subjective concerned with feelings and views.
Summative at the end; **evaluative** concerning examinations and accountability.
SWOT Strengths, Weaknesses, Opportunities, Threats is a technique for the systematic analysis of the school.

Further Reading

This further reading section is divided into an overall section followed by relevant chapter reading.

OVERALL

The following books are strongly recommended for additional reading:

Day, C., Johnston, D. & Whitaker, P. 1985 *Managing Primary Schools: A Professional Development Approach* PCP

Day, C., Whitaker, P. and Johnston, D. 1990 *Managing Primary Schools in the 1990s: A Professional Development Approach* 2nd Edition PCP.

Holly, P. & Southworth, G. 1989 *The Developing School* Falmer Press

Hopkins, D. 1989 *Evaluation for school development* Open University Press

OFSTED 1992 *The Handbook for the Inspection of Schools*

OFSTED 1992 *Framework for the Inspection of Schools*

Reid, K., Hopkins, D. & Holly, P. 1987 *Towards the Effective School* Blackwell

Southworth, G. 1987 *Readings in Primary School Management* Falmer Press

These books will also be useful as they have many relevant sections:

Beare, H., Caldwell, B.J. & Millikan, R.H. 1989 *Creating an Excellent School* Routledge

Hargreaves D. H. & Hopkins, D. 1991 *The Empowered School* Cassell.

HMI 1985 *Quality in Schools: Evaluation and Appraisal* HMSO

Hopkins, D. & Wideen, M. (Eds) 1984 *Alternative Perspectives on School Improvement* Falmer Press

Murphy, R. & Torrance, H. 1987 *Evaluating Education: Issues and Methods* PCP/OU

Nixon, J. 1992 *Evaluating the Whole Curriculum* Open University Press

Rodger, I.A. & Richardson, J.A.S. 1985 *Self-evaluation for Primary Schools* Hodder & Stoughton

Rogers, G. & Badham, L. 1992 *Education in Schools* Routledge

CHAPTERS

CHAPTER 1 THE CONTEXT FOR EVALUATION

Understanding the basic principles of evaluation.

Hughes, M., Ribbins, P. & Thomas, J. 1985 *Managing Education The System and the Institution* Holt, Rinehart & Winston

CHAPTER 2 WHOLE SCHOOL EVALUATION

External accountability

McCormick, R. (Ed.) 1982 *Calling Education to Account* Heinemann/OU

Nuttall, D.L. 1984 *School self evaluation: Accountability with a human face?* Longman for Schools Council

Stake, R.E. 1976 *Evaluating Educational Programmes* OECD

SBR—School Based Review

Hopkins, D. 1985 *School Based Review for School Improvement: A Preliminary State of the Art* Leuven, ACCO Belgium

Miles, M.B. & Ekholm, M. 1985 'What is school improvement?' in van Velzen, W.G., Ekholm, M., Hameyer, U. & Robin, D.
Making School Improvement Work ACCO Belgium

van Velzen, W.G., Ekholm, M., Hameyer, U. & Robin, D. 1985 *Making School Improvement Work* ACCO Belgium

GRIDS—Guidelines for Review and Internal Development in Schools

Abbott, R. *et al.* 1988 *GRIDS Primary School Handbook* 2nd edition Longman for SCDC

IMTEC

Dalin, P. *et al.* 1987 *School Development Guide* IMTEC/NFER

DION Elliott-Kemp, J. 1980 *Diagnosing Individual and Organisational Needs for Staff Development in Schools* PAVIC/Sheffield City Polytechnic

Critical Colleagues

Mountford, J. 1988 'The role of critical friends in school evaluation' *School Organisation* Vol. 8 No. 3 pp 255-260

Other methods

ILEA inspectorate 1977 *Keeping the School under Review* ILEA

Wiltshire County Council Paisey, A. & Paisey, A. 1977 *Effective Management in Primary Schools* Blackwell

CHAPTER 3 CLASSROOM BASED EVALUATION

Day, C., 1981 *Classroom-Based In-Service Teacher Education*

Shufflebeam, D.L. & Shinkfield, A.J. 1985 *Systematic Evaluation* Kluwer-Nijhoff, Boston

Index

More Books on Education Management

The following pages contain details of a selection of other titles on Education Management. For further information, and details of our Inspection Copy Service, please apply to:

Beyond the Core Curriculum

Co-Ordinating the Other Foundation Subjects in Primary Schools

EDITED BY
MIKE HARRISON

To help schools to meet the needs of the National Curriculum, primary teachers are required increasingly to act as consultants to their colleagues in particular subjects. This task of curriculum co-ordination often demands a new range of skills from teachers whose expertise may, hitherto, have been confined mainly to classroom teaching.

This practical book helps those charged with leading their school's staff in: Geography, History, Physical Education, Information Technology, Music, Art and Design, Technology, and Religious Education to develop their subject knowledge, network with others and find ways to influence colleagues to ensure that their subject is taught imaginatively and coherently in the school.

Written by a team of primary specialists this book offers invaluable advice and support to headteachers, teachers and students for whom the co-ordination of the foundation subjects in primary schools is an area of growing interest and responsibility.

The Editor, Mike Harrison, is Director of the Centre for Primary Education in the University of Manchester. He has worked as a primary teacher and a headteacher, leads primary pre-service education and is currently running inter-LEA courses for primary co-ordinators. He is known nationally for his courses on education management for prospective primary deputy heads. He is co-author of *Primary School Management* (Heinemann, 1992).

The ten co-authors are all primary experts in their fields, many running twenty-day training courses for primary co-ordinators in their subjects.

Paperback, 192 pages, tables.

The Language of Discipline

A practical approach to effective classroom management

BILL ROGERS

All teachers at some point in their careers encounter discipline problems in the classroom. Newly qualified and trainee teachers, in particular, often find classroom control the most demanding aspect of their new profession.

In this highly practical and user-friendly handbook Bill Rogers shows, step-by-step, how to draw up an effective discipline plan and strike the right balance between encouragement and correction. Good discipline does not just happen but is the product of careful planning, behaviour analysis, and the appropriate use of language and assertive skills. This book addresses all forms of disruptive behaviour, especially hostile and argumentative students, and shows that it is possible for every teacher, however inexperienced, to establish effective control and provide the right learning environment for the entire class. It will be welcomed by all teachers seeking a long-term positive solution to the demanding problem of disruptive behaviour in the classroom.

Bill Rogers is an education consultant specialising in classroom discipline and management, and teacher peer support. He was consultant to the *Elton Report: Discipline in Schools* (1989) and to the Victoria Ministry of Education (1985-88). He has taught at every level of education and written many articles and several books on discipline, teacher stress and teacher welfare including: *You Know the Fair Rule* (Longman, 1991), *Supporting Teachers in the Workplace* (Jacaranda, 1992), and *Making a Discipline Plan* (Nelson, 1989). He now lectures and runs INSET course in Australia and the United Kingdom where he is attached annually to the University of Cambridge Institute of Education to run in-service programmes on discipline and peer support for teachers.

Paperback, 176 pages, tables.

Managing Stress in Schools

A practical guide to effective strategies for teachers

MARIE BROWN & SUE RALPH

Managing stress is a growing problem for teachers in schools as they seek to meet the increasing demands of the National Curriculum, local management of schools (LMS), and the rising expectations of parents understandably wanting quantifiable examination results for their children approaching the highly competitive labour or higher education markets for the first time.

Based on sound psychological theory and research the emphasis of this book is, throughout, on practical solutions to teacher stress. Its sound analysis and realistic advice will enable teachers and those responsible for staff development both to identify the causes of stress, and to formulate a whole school policy for its management within the school.

Sue Ralph and Marie Brown both teach in the University of Manchester School of Education. They lecture and research in Educational Management and Administration, and Education and the Mass Media, and run inservice courses for teachers and other professionals. They have researched and published extensively on the effects of stress on teachers.

Paperback, 128 pages, tables.

Managing the Primary School Budget

An Introduction for Teachers and Governors

BRENT DAVIES & LINDA ELLISON

With the framework of the Local Management of Schools firmly in place, heads, staff and governors need to turn their attention to its implementation at the local school level.

This practical guide begins by establishing the key dimensions of LMS and reviews the nature of income and expenditure in the primary school. It moves on to a consideration of the way in which budgeting fits into school management development planning and examines the role of staff and governors in the process.

The book then adopts a step-by-step approach using a case study school to demonstrate how to go through the three key stages of budgetary review, planning and implementation. This will provide primary schools with a practical framework enabling them to manage their new-found financial responsibilities.

Brent Davies BA MSC teaches in the Centre of Education Management, Leeds Metropolitan University and is an LMS adviser to a large number of local education authorities. He has provided LMS management training for over 1000 primary heads in differing LEAS. He is the author of *Local Management of Schools* and a large number of articles on delegated finance. He is joint author with Linda Ellison of *Education Management for the 1990s.*

Linda Ellison MSc is a Senior Lecturer in charge of Education Management at Leeds Metropolitan University. She is extensively involved with programmes of senior management training, particularly for heads and deputies in primary schools. She has also been involved in the provision of staff development on LMS in a variety of LEAS. She is joint author with Brent Davies of *Education Management for the 1990s.*

> '...a simple, step-by-step guide through what can be a bewilderingly dense forest.' *Times Educational Supplement.*

Paperback, 128 pages, tables.

Marketing the Primary School

An Introduction for Teachers and Governors

BRIAN HARDIE

Schools have always had an eye on their 'reputation' and standing within the local community. However, open enrolment and competition for pupil numbers following the 1988 Education Reform Act have put a much greater value on the relationship which schools need to have with both parents and pupils. Now, in order to increase — and even maintain — pupil numbers, schools will be under much greater pressure to market themselves effectively. The author, who has been running courses in marketing and reputation management for primary school heads, shows how the primary school can be successfully promoted, stretching precious resources to make the most of contacts with the local community. Contents: Preface, the school in its marketplace, reputation management, marketing the school, meeting the customer, the prospectus and other communications, handling the media, further reading, useful addresses, glossary, index.

Brian Hardie MA DLC is a Senior Lecturer in Education Management at Crewe & Alsager Faculty of the Metropolitan University of Manchester, and runs courses in marketing and reputation management for primary school Heads. He is the author of *Evaluating the Primary School* (Northcote House, 1994).

> '... tells heads how to think the unthinkable... sound advice about things that good schools should have been doing for years...' *Times Educational Supplement.*
>
> 'The book works, as a handbook to be used and returned to as different activities are needed. The context and priority are right...the ingredients for the successful mix are right...the focus and presentation of the advice are simple and sharp.' *NAGM News.*

Paperback, 144 pages, illustrated.